///// Religion and the Public Good ///

///// Religion and the Public Good ///////////////
/// A Bicentennial Forum /////

with addresses by
William Lee Miller
Robert N. Bellah
Martin E. Marty
Arlin M. Adams

and with a foreword by
John F. Wilson

M/E/R/C/E/R

ISBN 0-86554-326-7

The paper used in this publication meets
the minimum requirements of American National Standard
for Information Sciences—Permanence of Paper
for Printed Library Materials, ANSI Z39.48-1984
∞

Library of Congress Cataloging-in-Publication Data
Religion and the public good :
a bicentennial forum /
with addresses by William Lee Miller . . . [et al.] :
and with a foreword by John F. Wilson.
 p. 139 15 x 23 cm. 6 x 9″
 ISBN 0-86554-326-7 (alk. paper)
 1. United States—Religion—Congresses. 2. Religion and state—United
States—Congresses. 3. Freedom of religion—United States—Congresses. 4. United States—Constitution—Congresses.
I. Miller, William Lee.
BL2525.R462 1988
323.44′2′0973—dc19   88-13667
                     CIP

323.442
R382
c. 1

//// CONTENTS ///

Old Christ Church Preservation Trust

The delegates to the Constitutional Convention who met in Philadelphia through the summer months of 1787 were desperate men. Their
overriding objective was to design a government better suited to the new
United States than were the Articles of Confederation, under which the
new nation had experienced so much difficulty. They elected to do their
work in private. Consequently, our knowledge of their discussions and
debates is circumscribed, and the result has been both speculative interpretations of what motivated the Founding Fathers as they met in
Carpenter's Hall and unwarranted assumptions as to their omniscience.

Such information as we possess clearly indicates that the delegates
directed little time or attention to the question of the relationship of religion to the proposed government. The document they eventually produced has but one clause explicitly referring to the subject, Article 6,
Section 3, which rules out religious tests for office holding in the new
federal government. The text says nothing further, except for being dated
"in the year of our Lord." As it enumerates federal powers and, for that
matter, those reserved to the states, the Constitution makes no explicit
mention of religious organizations, activities, or beliefs, just as it by-
passes numerous other subjects relevant to us (such as education or political parties).

As the various states reviewed the draft Constitution, they raised numerous objections to it, among them questions regarding the text's si-

lence on religion. Several states took the position that, without assurance of an attempt to remedy the shortcomings of the document, they would refuse to ratify. The First Congress, in considering how to mollify the states, included religion among the issues to be addressed. In the end, as we know, the two clauses regarding religion that emerged from the Committee of Conference between the Senate and House of Representatives, and that were eventually ratified as part of the First Amendment, specified that "Congress shall make no law respecting an establishment of religion, or prohibiting the free exercise thereof."

Read in the context of the founding of the United States, these clauses prohibited federal intervention in state practices with respect to religion, especially when those practices differed from those of the federal government. For example, some states continued to maintain "establishments," in the sense of requiring public funding of local churches; others required religious tests of candidates for office. Thus in their origin these clauses were, like the provision in Article 6, Section 3, exclusively limitations on the new federal regime. The First Amendment clauses were ruled applicable to the states and other levels of government only through the due process clause of the Fourteenth Amendment, in separate cases in the 1940s.

The virtual silence of the Constitution itself about religion, together with the paucity of reports about discussions in the convention, can be (and to some degree has been) construed as evidence that the Founders sought to construct a secular regime, one that would systematically separate church from state. The formulation of the First Amendment clauses as proposed and ratified may at least superficially lend support to the same conclusion. Thomas Jefferson's later metaphor of the "wall of separation," which he introduced in a letter to the Baptists of Danbury, Connecticut, only reinforces this presumption. If, therefore, we look at the circumstances under which the Constitution was drafted and, furthermore, consider that its single clause concerning religion and the two relevant clauses of the First Amendment were formulated to limit the federal government, we can see why they have been used to interpret the Constitution as an areligious, if not a secularistic, charter for the United States.

The bicentennial celebration of the Constitution is an appropriate time to reconsider this reading. What, indeed, was the role religion played in the new nation and in relation to its new government? If we return without prejudice to reanalyze the founding moment, a rather different picture begins to emerge. Far from being resolved to expunge religion, the delegates were, in fact, intensely aware of its importance. Religion in all its dimensions—individual and institutional, entailing behavior and belief, present in secular affairs, and simultaneously oriented to the sacred—was thoroughly a part of the social and cultural world they knew. Far from seeking to legitimate a new regime that would be antireligious or even indifferent to religion, they saw their objective as crafting a political structure that might survive the deep divisions, including those created by religion, that confronted them. The greatest threats to the new United States, in addition to hostile foreign imperial powers, were internal lines of division—for instance, between the several regions with their divergent economic interests and their different cultural patterns. Among the latter, religious differences were preeminent. On the basis of critical review, therefore, we must see religion as a prominent part of the range of social reality that contained the challenges facing the delegates meeting in Carpenter's Hall. We should be equally attentive to its importance in any assessment of the nation's later achievements.

We are fortunate that, as elaborate plans were being laid in Philadelphia to commemorate the two-hundredth anniversary of the signing of the draft Constitution, the present rector of Christ Church, the Reverend James Trimble, recognized an opportunity because of his church's close association with many members of the original convention. Believing that the place of religion in the United States, both at the founding moment and in the subsequent centuries, deserved special attention, he proposed that a program might be planned at this historic church that he served,[1] in concert with Philadelphia's major celebration of the Constitution itself. Such a program might explore the religious dimensions

---

[1] Christ Church is a magnificent building recently restored to reflect its condition in the late colonial and early national eras.

present in the nation's founding and, by extension, the continuing significance of religion to it. With the support of several individuals and foundations, an ambitious program of lectures, followed by responses on the part of distinguished guests, took place at the church on 4-6 October 1987.

Religion and the Public Good offers four lectures from that program, given by three well-known professional scholars and a highly respected jurist. Some of the responses to their presentations are also included. While not intended to address all relevant religious aspects of the bicentennial year, these lectures open for consideration many dimensions of the religious presence we have noted. Among the topics are perennial questions such as the relation of religious liberty to religiously sanctioned order, the interaction of religious ideas and political idealism, and the course to be charted through the vexing issues of church-state law at the end of the twentieth century.

William L. Miller picks up the theme of the place of religion in the penumbra surrounding the actual crafting and drafting of the Constitution. In comparing the American Revolution with the French, he notes the latter was enthusiastically enlightened in its commitments and that it simultaneously embodied strong antireligious impulses. By contrast, the American republic was created by individuals who retained their varied religious commitments. Above all, the American people—that ultimate reference point for the legitimacy of the new experiment—remained religiously active. In consequence, Miller emphasizes the confluence of religious traditions that created the culture of the new nation. And of all modern societies, that of the United States has continued most open to, and dependent upon, the religious vitality of its people.

Within the range of constituent religions he identifies, Miller gives primacy to the Puritan-Calvinist strand. Its proximate source was in the seventeenth-century civil struggles in England. But its intellectual development prepared the ground for, and proved consonant with, ''enlightened'' traditions that fostered the republican institutions fundamental to the new American nation. But while Miller assigns this priority to Puritanism, he also emphasizes the deep American dependence on other religious traditions as well, each of which has reinforced in its own way the essential impact that Puritanism has had upon the people and their representative government. In different ways, religious influences from Jewish, Catholic, Episcopal, Baptist, Methodist, and a host of other religious groupings, have made their own special contributions to the political organization of the United States.

Robert Bellah takes as his theme the contribution of religious language to the shape of public discourse. He strongly opposes a rigidly separationist reading of the American traditions of church and state. Indeed, he emphasizes that the First Amendment freedoms assure religion of its right to inform public discussion. Free exercise and free speech together buttress this central role for religious language in our polity, a role it has assumed, according to Bellah, from early colonial times. John Winthrop's lay sermon aboard the *Arbella,* which invoked the image of "the city on a hill," has direct sources in early Christian texts and deeper roots in those of ancient Israel. Moreover, Bellah believes that the master image of America as the kingdom of God has sustained and periodically renewed the central place the nation accords to religion.

While urging that the religious sources of American concepts of nationhood are clear, Bellah also explores the underside of this situation: our characteristic temptation to use an imperialistic idiom. Americans readily adopt language that makes universalistic claims about the nation and its mission while forgetting the principle of the transcendent judgment upon things human that is central to the language of faith. Thus religion "charges" the political order with extreme claims. For this reason, Bellah finds Reinhold Niebuhr's *The Irony of American History* to be of central importance. Niebuhr's criticism of America's pretensions to empire derives from and is sustained by religious traditions. Indeed, the image of a religious penumbra may contradict the central importance Bellah attributes to religious constructs in American culture. He insists that American public life is incomprehensible without attention to the religious terms, concepts, and idiom—whether taken as penumbral or focal—that have informed and suffused it. We may or may not think of ourselves as a religious people, but we are a people whose self-understanding has drawn directly and continuously on religious sources.

Bellah's estimate of the central place of religion in America at least implicitly raises a critical issue: Is religion free from governmental constraint? Does the United States protect and nurture religious freedom? For Martin E. Marty, this is a critical dimension of any consideration of "Religion and the Public Good," for the Founding Fathers constructed a federal polity that respected the free exercise of religion. This scheme denied established status to any and all religious groups. Indeed, it made religion subordinate to the political framework of the society. But this subordinate status in turn conferred the guarantee of freedom. Paradoxically, religion was lifted up and assured independence in the culture, although at the price of losing the established position the traditional churches of Europe had enjoyed vis-à-vis the state. Of course, this relationship has subtly transformed both religion and politics. As a result, Marty insists, religion in America is unique; consequently, any attempt at its analysis requires painstaking care.

Marty argues that this nontraditional resolution of the ancient European struggle between church and state is unsettling. In effect, it cuts America free from the moorings of acknowledged central values as a *consensus juris*. Thus, Americans find their society to be without a common core. And how can a nation whose scope and scale are effectively imperial survive without such a core? In characteristic fashion Marty turns the tables by asking, In what could such a consensus exist? The cultural effect of the republican ethos has been to diversify opinions and pluralize values to the point that it is impossible for us to imagine any simple core based on religious values that would gain general assent. Were there such a consensus, it could only be experienced as an "establishment," thus negating the religious liberty we prize.

The final major address in this book concerns the law. In the American constitutional tradition, the clauses of the First Amendment have been elaborated as the operational framework that situates religion and gives protection to its expression. Judge Arlin Adams's discussion begins with the interpretations of the First Amendment clauses in the last half century or so (until the 1940s, they were little developed in jurisprudence). With the *Cantwell* case (1940) and the *Everson* case (1947), respectively, the religious-liberty and establishment clauses were interpreted as constraining the states and even local levels of government through the due process clause of the Fourteenth Amendment. By means of this incorporation, provisions originally serving to limit federal action were applied as well to local and state governments. As for Article 6, Section 3, which ruled out religious tests for federal office, the Supreme Court ruled in *Torcaso* v. *Watkins* (1961) that, under the establishment clause, local officials could not be subject to such a test. The only provision in the original Constitution that directly concerns religion thus became effectively redundant.

In the half century during which the two First Amendment clauses have been interpreted, commentators have increasingly seen their interrelationships as vital. Each clause has proved capable of broad application—the one as a limit on governmental actions that might seem to entail establishing religion, the other as a restraint on actions that might abridge or circumscribe religious rights. Most of our other rights, like freedom of the press or of speech, stand alone. These religion clauses intersect, requiring accommodation between them. Judge Adams is especially interested in the potential for abuse arising from failure to respect the principles they articulate. He asserts that, while the application of each of these clauses is relatively well explored when they are taken singly, their interaction in particular cases creates a ''zone for permissible accommodation'' in which we shall need extensive case law in order to adjudicate the requirements of our religiously plural society.

Although it may seem a contradiction, the vigor and vitality of religion in the modern United States are related to its independence from regime. Thus religious groups and bodies have looked to their members for support rather than to governmental sponsorship and in doing so have come to exemplify the voluntary principle. The same principle underlies countless reform movements and social objectives that have developed from religious sources but have acquired independent life. Throughout the culture, religion, however formally distinct from government, has been critically important. And that culture has supported, sustained, and directed the American experiment through two centuries.

Readers of these essays and the responses will find a rich and varied fare. The objectives of the Christ Church Forum were to open for discussion large questions concerning religion and the public good. While the addresses published here all begin with and make reference to the

Constitution itself, to which religion was and is only indirectly related, they each make clear that religion has had continuing significance in American society for two hundred years. In this sense, they invite us to explore once again questions repeatedly asked and never finally answered. The forum has reminded us, in the context of the bicentennial celebration, of the enduring importance of these questions.

John F. Wilson

In the United States today, religion has been so privatized and po-
liticized that an honest exchange concerning the important role of religion in the life of this republic has almost been reduced to a cleric's
saying grace at public functions or to a television evangelist's running
for the office of president. In early 1986, when I was reviewing the various events proposed for the celebration of the two-hundredth anniversary of the signing of the Constitution of the United States, I was amazed
to find that not one proposal related to the importance of religion in the
founding of this form of government. In early May, therefore, I coned
the following group of distinguished scholars in the field of church-state
relations: John Wilson and Albert Raboteau of Princeton University,
Stanley Katz of the Woodrow Wilson School at Princeton, Jay Demer-
ath of the University of Massachusetts, and Robert Handy of Union
Theological Seminary. This group spent a day together and decided that
a conference dealing with the religious influences on the formation of
our Constitution would indeed be worth pursuing.

The ball was now in my court, and I persuaded the Old Christ Pres-
ervation Trust to sponsor such a conference. I chose the trust because I
wanted the conference to represent as ecumenical a stance as possible.
I wanted to include as speakers and responders men and women of letters, as well as clergy who represent diverse viewpoints. Work proceeded with the hiring of an executive director and the forming of an
advisory board. The board was carefully chosen to include clergy,

members of the bar, and academicians. They were mostly (but not all) from the Philadelphia area. The trust appropriated twenty-five thousand dollars, and Christ Church itself contributed five thousand dollars, to sponsor the conference.

Conference sessions were held in Christ Church on 4-6 October 1987 and included several prominent speakers and respondents whose contributions appear in this book. William Lee Miller, Miller Professor of Ethics and Institutions at the University of Virginia, considers the influence of religion on the writing of the Constitution. Responding to his presentation are Catherine Albanese, specialist in church-state relations, from the University of California; historian Sheldon Hackney, president of the University of Pennsylvania; and George Marsden, evangelical scholar and Professor of the History of American Religion, from Duke University.

Robert Bellah, whose book *Habits of the Heart* has provoked much discussion both within and outside the religious community, presents the second chapter in this volume. Bellah is currently Ford Professor of Sociology and Comparative Studies, University of California, Berkeley, and here considers the role of religion in public life. Respondents are Alida Brill, Russell Sage Foundation scholar; Robert Drinan, S.J., former congressman from Massachusetts and currently Professor of Law at Georgetown University; and Christopher Mooney, S.J., academic vice-president of Fairfield University and himself widely published on Bellah's topic.

Martin Marty, Fairfax M. Cone Professor of History of Modern Christianity at the Divinity School of the University of Chicago, considers the topic of church, state, and religious freedom. Marty, who may be the most well-known Protestant theologian in the United States today, examines related issues in depth in his recent book *Religion and Republic*. Robert Edgar, Methodist clergyman and former congressman from Pennsylvania, responds to Marty's chapter, as do Edmund Spaeth, Jr., retired president judge of the superior court of Pennsylvania, regarded as one of the finest judges in the state; and Jacqueline Wexler, president of the National Conference of Christians and Jews, an organization that has long championed the cause of religious freedom.

Finally, Arlin Adams, former distinguished judge of the United States court of appeals, examines the issue of religious pluralism—specifically, the doctrine of accommodation and the religious clauses of the Constitution. Adams is Jewish and is one of the most widely respected legal scholars in the country. Responding to his chapter are Robert DeWitt, former Episcopal bishop of Pennsylvania; Charles Douglas III, former senior justice on the New Hampshire Supreme Court, who has participated in many decisions relating to church-state issues; and John Wilson, Collord Professor of Religion at Princeton University, also experienced in church-state issues.

It is my hope that this book will reach both the church and the legal community. Perhaps it can serve as a model for an ongoing conference at Christ Church that will explore the meaning of citizenship and discipleship as we continue to ponder a religious person's response to the challenge of molding the world that God has given us.

James A. Trimble
Rector, Christ Church

WILLIAM MILLER

ROBERT BELLAH

MARTIN MARTY

ARLIN ADAMS

Religion and the Constitution

/// William Lee Miller ////

If we look at the body of the federal Constitution, as it was hammered out by Madison, Franklin, Wilson, and company in Philadelphia in the summer of 1787, we discover that the topic with which we are concerned is treated primarily (although not quite entirely) by negation, silence, exclusion, and inference. There is in this Constitution, in contradiction to many absentminded claims made by pious citizens of a later time, no formal commitment to Christianity, to belief in God, or to any religious belief whatsoever. The Constitution of the United States of America is not soaked in the explicit claims of Christian devotion, as, say, the constitution of Pakistan is soaked in the claims of Islam. The document that issued from the summer's work in Philadelphia made no religious affirmation, even of the conventional kind that was commonplace in documents written by the Founders: no references to the Creator, the Almighty, Providence, or the Supreme Being whom the Supreme Court would later say that the nation's institutions presuppose.

There was no appeal, as in the Declaration of Independence, to nature and nature's God; and no expression like the following, from state constitutions written later: "The people of Connecticut, acknowledging with gratitude the good providence of God, do . . . " (1818), or "We the people of the State of Arkansas, grateful to Almighty God for the privilege of choosing our own form of government . . . '' (1874). Perhaps the most interesting contrast is with the constitution of the *Confederate* States of America. The Confederate Constitution had of course many parallels to the U.S. Constitution, which the secessionists, as well as the unionists, revered. It is therefore the more interesting to see the changes. The rebels' preamble began thus: "We the people of the Confederate States, *each state acting in its sovereign and independent character.* . . . '' Although the purposes of this constitution parallel those of the U.S. Constitution and are expressed in the same language, the purpose to "promote the general welfare" was omitted. And then in the last line there was this *addition:* "invoking the favor and guidance of Almighty God."

But there was no such invoking in the U.S. Constitution. When the New York State Board of Regents, designing a program for piety and virtue in the schools, in the 1950s, referred to the belief in God reflected in not only the speeches of the Founders and other early documents but also in the U.S. Constitution, the skeptic might respond to this last: Where? The absence of any "acknowledgment of God" in the Constitution became an issue early in the nineteenth century, when Timothy Dwight at Yale, condemning the absence of any such acknowledgment as a disgrace, mounted a campaign to have that omission rectified. It was not successful, nor have been subsequent efforts to enact a "Christian amendment" (efforts that continue to this day). The formal charter of our national being makes no substantive religious affirmation, no collective religious commitment on the nation's behalf. We are not a "confessing" state.

The Constitution also includes no provision for the church's support, protection, or participation in national life. There were to be, under this American Constitution, no bishops in the House of Lords. No bishops in the established church sense—no bishops like the fictional Archdeacon Grantly in Anthony Trollope's novels, who waits anxiously upon the outcome of a parliamentary election to see whether he will be named, or like the real William Temple, whom Winston Churchill, though holding his nose, could not avoid naming archbishop of Canterbury. It is significant that we have no Lords Temporal, but it is even more significant that we have no Lord Spiritual.

In the late 1950s, in the midst of a discussion of "national purpose," the British prime minister, criticized for a pragmatism inade-
quately rising to the scope of the big picture, made a response that then
crossed the water to be told as though it were appropriate to the same
discussion in the United States: "If the people want a sense of national
purpose, let them get it from their bishops!" Very funny. It was the kind
of half-cynical deflationary comment loved by all journalists and most
modern politicians. But in the United States the people *have* no bishops
to get a national purpose, or anything else, from. There are Episcopal
bishops and Methodist bishops and Lutheran bishops and Catholic bish-
ops and many other kinds of bishops—but no bishops of the whole people, no bishops who can express with any kind of authority, to be
received with any kind of deference, a purpose for the whole nation.

Our forefathers of the revolutionary period had indicated, indeed,
how strongly they were opposed to any national, political, official bishops in the controversy just before the Revolution over the proposal to
send a Church of England bishop to America. So strong was the "an-
tiprelatical" bias of these Puritan-sectarian Americans that this "Great
Fear of Episcopacy" was a major cause of the shift in American opinion
toward revolution and independence, in a way that few Americans today even remotely understand and none can recapture. But for our purpose of reading the Constitution, I have used the symbol of the absence
of bishops simply as an indication of the larger point—the absence of
any formal provision for an ecclesiastical institution.

James Madison and his colleagues came to the position—a new one
in the political thought of the West—that in this republic *all* of the parts
and pieces of the complicated governmental machinery shall rest, in the
end, upon the whole and undivided people. In other words, it shall not
be, under this republic, that one house or part or organ of government
shall represent the one, another the few, another the many. Under this
Constitution there is no division of the realm into "estates," each of
which shall be constitutionally recognized and represented by a piece of
the governmental machinery. Neither is there the arrangement stem-
ming from more recent political theories—like those derived from the
papal encyclical *Rerum Novarum*—that reserves places in the constitu-

tional scheme for the mercantile and agricultural and seafaring interests, for lawyers and doctors, for each of the "industries and professions." There is no slicing of the body politic, of the whole people. *All* of the parts and pieces of the American constitutional system rest, in the end, through however many and complicated steps, upon the whole and undivided people. Even the Supreme Court, so many times in American history condemned for its nonmajoritarian resistance to the opinion of the day, rests in the end upon appointments by a president, who was to be chosen by electors, who were to be chosen by the whole people of a state; and this president's appointments are made with the advice and consent of the upper body of the federal Congress, the Senate, which in the beginning was to be chosen by the state legislatures, which then finally were chosen, again, by the whole people.

Among the estates that were thus eliminated from any formal place or recognition, any preferred or distinct representation or role, the most venerable was the ecclesiastical institution. Among the professions that were denied any distinct constitutional place, the most consequential was the clergy. Among the "opinions" (as Jefferson would call them) that were left free for each person's voluntary acceptance or rejection, without any shared commitment by the whole people in fundamental law, the most significant were opinions about religion. The church, the clergy, and Christian belief were all thrown out into the great sea of public discourse, to sink or swim altogether on their own, without any safety net whatsoever in the nation's fundamental law. Christianity was cut free from all formal collective support in a way that, in Europe, it had not known since the emperor Constantine raised the banner of the cross as the insignia of the Roman state.

No collective commitment, no state-supported church—and no religious test for public office. The one significant explicit reference to religion in the body of the Constitution is the provision at the end of Article 6 that "no religious test shall ever be required as a qualification to any office or public trust under the United States"—very important in its own time, almost forgotten in ours. In the Constitutional Convention North Carolina's delegation opposed the provision in Article 6, because it might allow "pagans and Roman Catholics" to hold office—as indeed it has.

This provision and the rejection of all titles and nobility were the features that persuaded Isaac Backus, the most important of Separate Baptist clergymen, or the pietists, to support ratification of the Constitution in Massachusetts and to urge his fellow Baptists and other dissenters to do likewise. No religious test; no *requirement* that one profess any tenant of religion in order to be a legislator, a president, or even a notary public; no required religious profession in order to hold a public office and, by extension, to be a voter, a citizen, a member with standing equal to that of every other in the polity.

Throughout Western history, including the experience of all the American colonies at one time or another, there had been such tests: excluding Jews from office virtually everywhere, excluding Catholics in Protestant states, excluding Protestants in Catholic states, excluding Quakers, excluding Unitarians, and of course excluding atheists, agnostics, and "free thinkers" everywhere. The first South Carolina state constitution required a belief in the "Protestant Christian Religion"; tolerant Maryland required belief in the Trinity; more tolerant Pennsylvania required a belief in God. Reading in the history of colonial Virginia, one is startled to discover a requirement that potential officeholders swear that they do *not* believe in transubstantiation in the mass—a specific searching out of Catholics for exclusion. All of the colonies except Roger Williams's Rhode Island and, after the passage of Jefferson's Statute, Virginia, had some sort of religious oath for officeholders still in the revolutionary period. So the prohibition in Article 6 was no small thing. It was part of the same enlightenment and dissenting project, to sweep away, at last, the terrible history of state-enforced exclusions, preferences, and even persecutions that had marked the 1,400-year history of state-supported Christianity.

Surely the actual and symbolic meaning of the prohibition against religious tests must have played a large role in the decisions made by millions of Europeans in the nineteenth and early twentieth centuries—from Ireland, Italy, Poland, Russia, and every other country of Europe—to make the arduous journey across the Atlantic to settle in this new "empire of liberty." James Madison was no phrase maker, but even he bordered on eloquence when he argued, back in 1784, in favor of "that generous policy, which, offering an asylum to the persecuted and oppressed of every nation and religion, promised lustre to our country.''

More than 170 years later, in September 1960, one descendent from ''that generous policy'' was the Democratic candidate for president, who ''happened to be a Catholic.'' Two of his assistants, Theodore Sorensen and the late John Cogley, working on a speech to be given to Baptist and other preachers in Houston, made relentless use of a tactic we might call the rhetoric of bait-and-switch. (One believes *A;* therefore one must concede its parallel, *B.*) They made potent use of that device, in particular, with respect to the constitutional provisions respecting religion: ''I would not look with favor,'' said candidate John Kennedy, ''upon a president working to subvert the First Amendment's guarantees of religious liberty. . . . And neither do I look with favor upon those who would work to subvert Article 6 of the Constitution by requiring a religious test—even by indirection.''

Kennedy then went on to challenge his Protestant interlocutors in Houston actually to overturn the prohibition in Article 6, if that was their effective position. ''For if they disagree with that safeguard, they should be openly working to repeal it.''

In the next year, 1961, the United States Supreme Court decided the case *Torcaso* v. *Watkins,* in which a Maryland ''unbeliever'' named Torcaso declined to swear his belief in God, as he was required to do in order to hold the office of notary public. Although the case was decided in Torcaso's favor on the basis of the First Amendment's establishment clause, his lawyers appealed against the Maryland law requiring a belief in God, to Article 6 of the federal Constitution. (Parenthetically, we may note that this was the case in which Justice Hugo Black adopted, into a footnote in the Court's opinion, from a submission by the noted church-state advocate Leo Pfeffer, a list of religions that do not affirm a belief in God. Besides Buddhism and Confucianism, the list unfortunately included the phrase *secular humanism;* the reading by conservative religionists of the footnotes in Supreme Court cases seems to be one source, at least, of the construct that has come to play a major role in later events. Leo Pfeffer has written that he is sorry he ever mentioned the term.)

The overwhelmingly most important provision of the Constitution with respect to religion was still to come, when the thirty-nine Founders present and willing to sign the Philadelphia constitution affixed their signatures on 17 September 1787. Already at that moment there was grumbling because the document contained no bill of rights; George Mason, the Virginia gentleman who we might call the human-rights advocate of that time, having failed in a last-minute effort to attach a bill of rights in Philadelphia, declined to sign, went grumpily home, and opposed ratification. Thomas Jefferson in Paris objected to the absence of a written bill of rights, and that objection was a prominent theme in the campaign of the antifederalists against ratification.

In contrast to the present time, when religious freedom (something like "freedom to go to the church of one's choice") is rather far down the list of freedoms the broad public cares about, long after economic freedom and some kind of "expression," eighteenth-century Americans who wanted a written bill of rights cared most of all about religious liberty—freedom of "conscience," as they would put it. The "contagion of liberty," in Bernard Bailyn's term, spread the fever of freedom to the struggle against state restrictions on religious beliefs and against established churches. Dissenting Protestants were prominent among those who insisted, in the argument over ratification, that a written bill of rights be added to the Constitution and were among those to whom the proratification people like James Madison made their promise that *after* ratification such a bill would be introduced, a promise fulfilled by Madison in the First Congress, in 1789. When the first ten amendments were ratified in 1791, the foundations of the new American church-state arrangement were in place.

The first clauses of what came to be the First Amendment dealt with religion. The "free exercise" clause, as it would come to be called, picked up the phrase that the young James Madison had used in his amendment of the Virginia Declaration of Rights back in 1776. It was joined to and preceded by the rather curious establishment (or no-establishment) clause ("Congress shall make no law respecting an establishment of religion"), which waits there for courts and judges and constitutional lawyers much later to chop and blend and splice and spread, the clause that has been taken to signify our tradition of separating church and state.

The prohibition against religious tests in Article 6 was very important in its own time but has become much less so in our time; with the establishment clause the situation is reversed. Since the Supreme Court decisions of the late 1940s, it has exploded in significance in the United States, very different from that seen by James Madison.

The individual states meanwhile worked out their new constitutions and their bills of rights too; the Virginia Statute was quite influential on those developments. The state establishments still in existence at the time the Constitution was written were thereafter abolished, the last ones being New Hampshire in 1817, Connecticut in 1818, and Massachusetts in 1833. By that time, as de Tocqueville had observed, the "voluntary way" in religion had so completely triumphed in the American mind that he could find nobody who disagreed with it.

The American Constitution thus reflected these great national negatives on the subject of religion: no common confession, no state-recognized church, no required belief for holding office, and no state interference with the freedom of opinion in matters of belief. In some quarters in Europe it may have been concluded that the constituting of the new nation represented at least a liberating disengagement from, perhaps even a hostility to, the long Christian tradition of the West. In the ten years since it was written, European scholars, and philosophers, and literati (in Jefferson's own assessment) had greeted Jefferson's Bill for Establishing Religious Freedom with "infinite approbation," propagated it with enthusiasm, translated it into French and Italian, inserted it in the Encyclopedia and other publications where America was mentioned, and circulated it in the courts of Europe.

Perhaps these enlightened Europeans had concluded that that thrilling document of Jefferson's had meant that across the Atlantic this new land declaring its independence now from the European past was going to realize what they, these enlightened Europeans, in their own countries, thought to be necessary: a repudiation of the Christian past, with all its cruelties and restrictions on the freedom of the mind. Perhaps they would conclude that this Philadelphia Constitution, continuous with that great Virginia document from their friend Jefferson, represented, at last, in this new nation, what they sought in Europe: freedom from religion!

Liberation from the "shackles" (a favorite word of Jefferson's) on the mind, the obscurantism, the social oppression of the religious past. Perhaps they would have expected therefore that, in this constituting of the first new nation, this making of a *Novus Ordo Seclorum,* a new order of the ages, there would be a new counting of the year's calendar, because the world was begun anew. The French in 1791 would institute a new calendar dated from the autumnal equinox, the day after the republic was proclaimed.

But look again at what these Americans *did* do, in their constitution. When in September 1787 they came to the end of their constitution, with its great implicit and explicit emancipating negatives with respect to religion, they dated it "in the year of our Lord seventeen hundred and eighty-seven, and of the independence of the United States the twelfth."

When they provided, in the body of the document, for a counting of days for a presidential veto, they exempted Sunday; they certainly did not even consider constructing, as did the French for a brief time, a new weekly cycle, abolishing the Christian Sabbath and replacing it with a new festival every tenth day. Exempting Sunday! "In the year of our Lord"! These customary items are minor, to be sure—these little differences between the French and the American revolutions—and yet they are also major.

Although the American Founders accomplished the Enlightenment and "democratic" goal of a full religious liberty to a degree unique in Christendom, at the same time, in sharp contrast to the other great overturning spawned by the Enlightenment, and perhaps in contrast to subsequent revolutionary events in nineteenth-century Europe, the Americans did not regard their Revolution as a repudiation of the Christian past. Their "new order of the ages" was not *that* new. They did not set the new republic over against the old Christianity. Within the Constitution itself in these minor ways the Americans did not repudiate, but rather acknowledged and continued, the overwhelmingly Christian heritage out of which they had come. And those little symbols within the Constitution itself stood for characteristics of the new nation that were very important outside it, in the life and culture of the new Americans.

It was no part of the Americans' "revolutionary" purpose, in constructing this new nation, to make a break with the long history of Christendom. The Americans, unlike the Europeans, explicitly disentangled themselves from monarchy, explicitly repudiated aristocracy and hierarchy, implicitly repudiated priesthood, and set in place a new nation with liberty and equality at the center, without casting the Christian religion as any kind of opponent. So Christianity, the great muddy Mississippi of Western civilization, was able, almost uniquely in the American setting, to flow unvexed to the sea of modern democratic life.

The United States managed to come into being as a modern democratic state with the connection with its Christian past unbroken and undamaged. This nation was born free, and did not have to become so; it was born Protestant, and did not have to become so. Although it had much, and was to acquire much more, of the religious history of Europe within the collective memory of segments of its population, it did not have with its own common national memory any Reformation or Counter-Reformation, any massacres, martyrs, or religious wars.

It did not even have a Restoration. America, the land of constructive Protestantism, was primarily the land of constructive *Puritan* Protestantism. Here in these colonies that particularly energetic form of Protestant Christianity, the Puritan movement of sixteenth- and seventeenth-century England, came through into the modern world more nearly intact and purer than in the Mother Country herself. Here there was no "Puritan" civil war (as it used to be called), no beheading of a king, with all of its traumas, no Puritan commonwealth, no Cromwell, and no Cromwellian massacre of Irish Catholics in Ireland. Here then, also, there was no Restoration, with its repudiation of the spirit and practice of the Puritans. The mind draws back from the concept of a Merrie *New* England. There had never been one; there was no moment to return to it if there had been.

Moreover, Puritanism in the United States did not have the Anglican and Catholic prior presence to contest the soil with it, as it did in old England; here Puritanism had a culture to build, afresh, of its own. And so also with the Great Awakening of the 1740s, which was not confined to the American colonies but part of a worldwide evangelical revival: on this side of the Atlantic it had fewer and less entrenched opponents and competitors. And so also yet again with the so-called

Second Great Awakening, the waves of revivals early in the new nation's life, in the early part of the nineteenth century, which penetrated deep because the alternatives were fewer and the sympathetic preparation greater than in other lands of Christendom.

The culture of the United States was to be much affected—one might almost say formed—by three religious movements (three Christian, Protestant movements) of unusual intensity: the Puritan movement of sixteenth- and seventeenth-century England and America (Perry Miller wrote that one cannot, for good or ill, understand America without understanding Puritanism), the Great Awakening of the 1730s and 1740s (which H. Richard Niebuhr called "our national conversion"), and the Second Great Awakening of the first half of the nineteenth century (which, in my opinion, American historical scholarship has not yet adequately assimilated). The adherents and heirs of each of these three interwoven movements, two before and one after the founding of the nation, certainly did not regard their religious faith as in any way contrary to the core meaning of the new nation.

To say that Christianity flowed relatively unperturbed into the modern American nation would be, for many Americans, only the minimal and negative aspect of a major and positive fact. For them the Christian religion did not simply manage to remain intact in the new country—it flourished, it was fulfilled, it almost realized its earthly program. Many Americans could regard the Revolution and Constitution making not only as wholly compatible with but as a divinely inspired expression of the claims of the Christian belief. Isaac Backus used the term *second Reformation* for what others called the American Revolution. It was to him a great *religious* event. "Religious liberty" was for him and for other Separate Baptist leaders a positive religious theme, foremost indeed among their beliefs: it meant freedom, at last, to preach, to hear and believe, and to act upon the gospel. The "black regiment" of clergy supporting the revolutionary cause, to which James Otis referred, undoubtedly also conceived that cause in high religious terms.

Perry Miller, in his article "From the Covenant to the Revival," assembled an impressive array of quotations from pastors not just from New England but from throughout the colonies who apply the ancient form of the Puritan jeremiad to the revolutionary struggle of the American colonials, linking denunciations of the covenanted people's sins with confidence that God will come to the covenantial people's aid. " 'Rationalism' was never so widespread,'' wrote Perry Miller, "as liberal historians, or those fascinated by Jefferson, have imagined. The basic fact is that the Revolution had been preached to the masses as a religious revival.'' The Deists, Richard Niebuhr wrote, furnished the American Revolution most of the brainpower, but the believing masses furnished the troops.

As the founding events of this modern republic did not represent a repudiation of the Christian past, so also they did not divide the people along a lasting and consistent religious fault line, as the modern and democratic revolutions of Europe characteristically were to do. There were not to be, and there are not now (as John Courtney Murray remarked), two Americas, as there are two Frances, two Spains, two Italys.

In the United States the religious reactionaries and conservatives were not systematically antirepublican; and the radicals and reformers were not systematically antireligious. Most of the former group were Tories, like Jonathan Boucher, preaching from his Church of England pulpit, sometimes with pistols on it, in favor of order and deference and loyalty to king and country (that is, England), and against the Revolution and the patriots. But Boucher ended his life in England, as did thousands of Tories and Loyalists, opponents of the American patriot cause, who fled to Nova Scotia or elsewhere in Canada and back to England. Many of them presumably were devout; certainly a great many were politically conservative Anglicans; it is said that one-third of the Church of England clergy in the American colonies fled during the revolutionary period. Obviously such an exodus removed from the new America an element that would have created a different religiopolitical mixture, had it remained within the nation, as something like it happened in European countries despite many fleeings and many murderings. In United States history, the politically reactionary religious element was left behind *twice:* by the Puritans, leaving it behind geographically in England and the Continent when they sailed across the Atlantic; and by the patriots, leaving it behind ideologically, when they declared independence.

On the other side, then, the radical, reformist, republican, revolutionary component of the colonial American population did not see religion as a systematic enemy of the new nation and the new order they were bringing into being. Although major leaders of the American founding can be said to have been a part of, or much influenced by, the Enlightenment—Thomas Jefferson, Benjamin Franklin, perhaps Jefferson's friend James Madison, and even John Adams, the New Englander who was also a Puritan in many ways—these American Enlightenment revolutionaries did not regard hanging the last king in the entrails of the last priest as part of their revolutionary program. Although an American leader, Thomas Jefferson, could regard the revolution as a repudiation of the rule of kings, priests, and nobles, such persons were all conveniently elsewhere.

Although the Revolution and the founding, in the atmosphere of the international Enlightenment, did generate a "religion of reason," a "republican religion," with a certain popular following, and some well-known leaders like Ethan Allen, the hero of Ticonderoga, and Joel Barlow, the Connecticut wit, and Elihu Palmer, who published a journal called *The Temple of Reason,* and although a great many of the wagons heading west in the new country no doubt carried a copy of Tom Paine's vigorous repudiation of orthodox Christianity, *The Age of Reason,* a great many *more* wagons, no doubt, carried a copy of the Bible. The adherents of the republican religion fought in the Revolution and disputed in the ratification debates, alongside New Light products of the awakenings, Old Side Presbyterians, standing order Congregationalists, and Anglican gentlemen.

There was in America, to put it mildly, no consistent identification of religion, or of Christianity, with reaction, with the Tories, with the feudal or monarchial or aristocratic resistance to a new "republican" government. Religion and "liberty" were not opposed to each other. Thomas Jefferson, from reading too many books in Paris, might in one corner of his brain think that way, but very few other Americans did, and the structure of national life went against it. For Americans in their civic capacity, religion was not perceived to be opposed to republican government. For believing Americans in their religious capacity, liberty, republicanism, and the new nation under the Constitution were not perceived to be inimical to the Christian church or Christian beliefs. Far from it. No confessing state—and "in the year of our Lord." No religious test—and a believing people. No established church—and a Christian culture.

The United States was unusual as measured by the European *past* in its radical break with the state church and in its provision of full religious liberty. It was to be unusual measured against the European *future* in the degree to which Christianity persisted and penetrated the culture. These two ways of being unusual have seemed to many Americans, perhaps to most, not at all to be contradictory, or even in tension with each other, but mutually reinforcing. And so there came into being then an unusual nation in which from the beginning, down to the foundation, and all the way across the culture, Christianity and liberty, Christianity and republicanism, were not enemies but friends.

We have been identifying the explicit constitutional provisions about religion and have discovered that there are not many to consider. One might as well refer to the *absence* of such provision. But these explicit institutional connections or disconnections, these silences, and these formal protections and negations in the Constitution itself are not, of course, the only way that religion is related to the American federal Constitution. There is also the realm of the *ideas* upon which the Constitution rests, implicit in its formulations. In its implicit understanding of humankind, in its social theory, does this constitutional system reflect the Christian tradition? or a particular branch of the Christian tradition?

It has been said that it does—in the "checks and balances" and "pluralism" that are its theoretical underpinnings. The understanding of life, of humankind, and of the world on which these rest was to be found (so it was said) in the Reformed Christianity that was overwhelmingly the dominant religious movement in the colonies. This quotation from Lord Bryce was once widely known: "There is a hearty Puritanism in the view of human nature that pervades the instrument of 1787. It is the work of men who believed in original sin, and were resolved to leave open no door which they could possibly shut."

The principle of checks and balances extends from government on out into the theory of our society, as one can see by reading James Madison, particularly *Federalist 51*. And that theory—of the desirable results of diversity in a people who have a prior unity—can be extended from interests to ideas; it can be linked to theory that underlies our freedoms of speech and the press and—most fundamentally—religion. Now, after two hundred years of experience with our founding principles, we still say that there is benefit in diversity. It is with reference to religion, in fact, that the whole theory began.

Shutting the door to human sinfulness, checking everybody and balancing everything, though very important, is not the only or the first principle of our constitutional government: the Articles of Confederation, in its way, had that. Those principles, taken *alone,* lead to chaos or tyranny. Prior to the restraining and the balancing, there is the grant of the power that is to be restrained; it is the putting together of these two, and not the checks and balances only, that is the genius of our Constitution. And in order for the two to be combined—to grant power and to restrain power—there must be a prior commonality, a coming together of the people into one. It has been said that the most important phrase in the Constitution is the first one in the preamble: "We, the people of the United States." The premise that there *was* a people, *one* people, separated now from others—from England—and united into a single unit, is the foundation of the whole. That balancing takes place within a prior and supervening mutual engagement, without which it would be, and is, meaningless or dangerous. This mutual engagement is an agreement to each other to make one people and to serve the shared good, and to seek and define it by mutual persuasion, by endless deliberation.

The two bodies of constitutional ideas that Americans have vaguely in their heads—one that clusters around the phrase *checks and balances* and another that clusters around various phrases for civil freedoms, *free speech* perhaps most of all—are not separated but joined. One can see the common matrix in a Puritan tract like Milton's *Areopogitia* and in the political writing that comes out of Puritan-Federalist-Covenant theology, especially as it is affected by the sectarians to the left. Not only is each of us restrained by the other, but also from the interchange (at its best) there comes something better than from any one of us.

This understanding of our social and political life arose in large part with reference to religious squabbles. So what did this country, which reflected that understanding, become?

Partly from luck and partly from principle, it developed a unique religious pluralism, the full effects of which we are just comprehending now, after two hundred years. (It has been masked from us until recently by the long Protestant cultural domination.) In the nation's beginning none of the great partners to the conversation in the West was in principle excluded, and none was decisively and officially dominant.

I have said already that the American achievement of nationhood and republican government under the Constitution in no way represented a triumph of modern enlightened reason over ancient unrepublican obscurantist religion. Nor did this achievement involve the triumph of one church or kind of religion over another.

Although the religious institutions of all these hitherto English colonies had some tie, however remote, to the established Church of England (even as the patriots rebelled against the England it was the church of), and although some of the Anglican clergymen, with their ordination oath of loyalty to the king, remained loyal to England, some of them fleeing to Canada and back to England, there was nevertheless no permanent division of the new American public along any Anglican/non-Anglican line. In fact, the very greatest leaders of the whole founding period, the writer of the great revolutionary document the Declaration of Independence, the leading architect of the Constitution, and above all the hero who presided at the Philadelphia convention and became the new nation's first president were all Anglican laymen. Although the Church of England suffered in the revolutionary and founding era, it emerged safely on the other side as the Episcopal church, one ''denomination'' alongside the others in the new nation.

The more significant case, in this land of constructive Protestantism, was the Roman Catholic church, whose political role had figured in all of those bifurcations in the nations of Continental Europe. Although a great many of the new Americans in this overwhelmingly Protestant country, born in the Enlightenment springtime of modernity, would regard the Roman Catholic church as an enemy of republican government (there is even in the very Declaration of Independence itself a veiled attack upon the Quebec Act, with the premise that Catholicism is an enemy of republican institutions), the Catholic church itself, Maryland and the Carroll family notwithstanding, was not an institutional presence in the new nation's politics, nor identified with the immediately relevant enemies of the emerging republic. Catholic France was an ally against Protestant England. Such Catholics as there were (like the Carrolls) were patriots, too.

The more severe, nativist anti-Catholicism that would come later, that has marred American history, and that became particularly virulent in the middle of the nineteenth century (enough so to help to generate a separate political party) was nevertheless always counterbalanced by the more generous and inclusive understanding that is there in the nation's founding documents. At best, the Americans knew that nativism and anti-Catholicism were contrary to the nation's constitutional morality. If the Illinois lawyer Billy Herndon, like many other hinterland Americans of the nineteenth century, had an abiding prejudice against Irish Catholics, his equally midwestern law partner had a different and better view, grounded, as he said with unparalleled eloquence, in the nation's original meaning, a meaning he did more than any other person to define and complete.

If neither Roman Catholicism nor any other religious body or movement could be decisively cast as a permanent enemy of America's republicanism, neither could "secularism," or irreligion, or as it was called then, "infidelity." It is important to underscore this point. Of course, some of the pious, especially as the evangelical America emerged in the nineteenth century, tried to make that interpretation (as some evangelicals try to do today), but in the long run and throughout the whole culture, their interpretation could not and cannot prevail. Such an interpretation would see the founding of America unequivocally as a triumph of religious faith over infidelity, of believers over unbelievers, of religion over irreligion. The Enlightenment, with its edge of skepticism, was too much present in the Revolution, in the new nation's institutions, in key founders, perhaps in the mind of the people—and, in effect, in the Constitution itself—for that view to be persuasive. So was the principle of liberty, derived partly from Christian sources but partly from other sources.

If the American Revolution differed in many ways, and perhaps fundamentally, from the French, it also overlapped with it enough for the two to be paired as the democratic revolutions that inaugurated the modern age. If many Christians of the sorts that predominated in the American colonies came to believe in "free institutions," and if the origins of such institutions can in considerable part be found in the left-wing of the Puritan Revolution, it is nevertheless doubtful that the Christian tradition *alone* would ever have generated, from within itself, a fully articulated free society, a new republic, a "democracy." Another great movement—republicanism, the Enlightenment—to some degree outside the Christian tradition, was necessary to achieve that result.

And those great silences, negations, and protections of the Constitution stood there preventing any closed and final "religious" interpretation of the nation's essence—any interpretation, that is, that would shut the door on the "free thinkers" who fled to this country in hope, on "secular humanists," who found in democracy their faith, on the various forms of unbelief, quasi-belief, and amiable indifference that this nation welcomed and spawned.

When the great Connecticut church leader Lyman Beecher headed West to save the frontier from two enemies, infidelity and popery, he did not succeed in either of those negative purposes, but he and his fellow evangelists did succeed in their positive purpose: the evangelization of the American West. By its silences and negations and its sotto voce affirmations, the U.S. Constitution shaped the possibility of such a result—in Beecher's day and in ours. We cannot extirpate those "enemies"; we cannot bind the whole people to one cluster of answers to questions of ultimate meaning. But we can tap, and help to shape, the underlying spiritual continuities of this nation with a soul of a church. By its silences, negations, and protections the Constitution affirmed, in this field as in others, equality and liberty—with respect to religion, perhaps best expressed a century and a half earlier by Roger Williams's term *soul freedom*.

If the United States had no permanent religious enemies to its nationhood or its republicanism, it also had no unequivocal or exclusive champions, even though there were many claimants. If a big American freshman religion class would write about the denominations, the instructor grading these papers would find that virtually every denomination would claim for itself a central place, even *the* central place, in the foundations of the American nation. The criteria for centrality would shift, of course, with each appraisal. The Baptists would explain that Roger Williams and religious freedom was the foundation stone of the distinct American institutions. The Presbyterians would write that the American form of government, representative and tripartite, was molded on the Presbyterian, and that the Constitution is full of a Calvinist and Reformed-Puritan-Presbyterian sense of the need to check human sinfulness. The Congregationalists would find the American pattern set by the Puritan Congregationalists and the New England town meeting.

The Catholics would broaden the lens and write that the whole structure of the American proposition rests upon Catholic natural law, which Jefferson got from Cardinal Bellarmine; they would reach out to the French Catholic American and Spanish Catholic American that would one day be joined to English Protestant American. The Methodists would write that Methodism, conquering the American West and South with an active practical idealism, would become so central to the American ethos that the day would come when President Theodore Roosevelt would say he felt he was nearest to the heart of America when he attended a Methodist convention. The Episcopalians might write that all of the original American colonies and almost all the colonists had a fundamental tie to the Church of England—not only the established Anglican churches of the southern colonies, but the Puritans of New England as well. The Unitarians, having read a book by A. Powell Davies, would explain that the Deist-Unitarian heritage, shared by Paine, Jefferson, Lincoln, and most other important American leaders, is the true religion of America. And so on. What Mormon or Christian Science students might write, it has not been within my experience to learn. Jewish students—I expand a little now to later experiences, beyond the classroom—might have written that, although there were scarcely any actual Jewish persons present in the American founding, something more important was: the *book* was there, undergirding everything in this new

American Israel, this almost-chosen people. There can be a cornerstone in almost every corner.

If these claims have varying degrees of plausibility, none wholly wrong, they are also, none of them, wholly right, insofar as they may implicitly exclude the others and close the door. The same reservation against monopolistic and exclusive claims by particular religious bodies applies, of course, to broad religious movements, theological tendencies, philosophical positions, social, moral and political applications, forms of devotion, ritual, and action that cut across, and in much of American history have been more important than, the formal denominational lines. Consider, for example, the claims about national origins and norms made by the conservative religiopolitical movement that became visible in the middle 1970s: that the nation was founded on belief in God, as part of "God's plan," and that the Puritans (interpreted, wrongly, to have been evangelicals and fundamentalists) are the whole story of America's essence and beginning. When those sorts of claims are made, one needs to be reminded again not only of the religious diversity of the colonies but also of the major role in the American founding of the Enlightenment, of Deism, even of a certain skepticism about and emancipation from religious claims.

On the other hand, when the modern-day heirs of the Enlightenment, who occupy most of the seats of power and influence in twentieth-century America, claim or more often just assume that their religionless outlook is *the* foundation of America, that opinion needs to be challenged, too. Such a position or attitude did play an important role, but the history of the Christian West, and the particular forms of Christian belief in the American colonies, played a very important role, too.

The United States was created by a great and complex mingling of movements. These movements were themselves mingled internally. Republicanism, constitutionalism, the Enlightenment, and classical civic humanism overlapped with each other and with the more distinctively religious strands of thought. Christianity had come out of, and taken up into itself, much of its parent Judaism. Then in its Catholic version, it had taken up into itself much from the classical world that the "republican" world was also recovering. In its Protestant version, the Christianity that helped to form America had interacted with the other forces making the modern world. Declaring from whence intellectually and spiritually the United States sprang is thus not so easy a task as partisans imply.

I have already said, perhaps with a touch of partisanship of my own, that one should not underestimate the role played in this complicated drama of our national spiritual and intellectual origins by the Puritan-Protestant-Christian-biblical component. Exactly from the fortunate mingling, and not from the exclusive contribution of any one of the parties, arose the distinctive merit of this remarkable nation. Both in our national origins and ideally today, the several parties may become less threats to and rejections of each other than they are complements to and correctives of each other.

That mutualism includes certainly the relationship of the religious parties to the Enlightenment and the "secular" republican parties—they needed, influenced, corrected, and complemented each other. They did so in the making of the American Constitution and can do so today. Moreover, as I have said, they were—and are—not all that neatly separated.

They affected each other internally as an influence, and not simply externally as a rival power unit. As that fortunate implicit and largely inadvertent collaboration between a Puritan-Protestant movement and an Enlightenment, secular republican movement worked together (in an intellectual and spiritual collaboration, not in any overt political alliances) without either of them exactly intending to create the foundations of this nation, so we should attempt to mold the same kind of mutually invigorating pluralism among the much wider spread of parties to the great conversation in the contemporary United States.

Our forefathers in the founding era and the forefathers of our forefathers in the Puritan and the republican tradition thought deeply about how people who differ about life's premises may nevertheless live together in peace and unity and service to the common good. Their thought on that question (essentially, the question of religious liberty) was the underpinning for the great themes of our Constitution: freedom of speech; freedom of the press; limited government under law; checks and balances; we, the people; out of many, one.

Our problem today, despite some echoes and shrill statements, is not the same as that of either of these sets of forefathers. Indeed, the shrill statements and the thoughtless echoing of past formulas, both by the religious right and by their most visible opponents, add to our different, present problem. For the forefathers the primary problems were disunity, fanaticism, and persecution. For us the problem is shallowness. The toleration and the freedom that they achieved and bequeathed to us as the solution to their problems may, if improperly understood, aggravate ours. For them, liberty was not a claim *against* society but a condition *of* society. Liberty therefore implied balanced and reciprocal duties. The mutual deliberation of parliamentary government, now institutionalized in the Congress that was at the center of the Constitution they produced, was not derided with disdain for "politicians" but was understood to be a great achievement in the history of human governance. The great underlying principle of benefits deriving from diversity within a people who are one was by no means to be taken for granted, treated on the surface only, but understood to be an accomplishment of great difficulty, because the diversities were real and deep.

In our own century John Courtney Murray described the United States as a united people in whom the great "conspiracies" of Western history appear "locked in argument." Our deliberation about first principles, about life's ultimate premises, is not subordinate, superficial, or of no consequence but is (or may be) substantial, in its substantive particularity constitutive of the national being of this remarkable people. In its deep implications our Constitution shows us to have come (1) out of Christian history and to be many, one, and free; (2) out of the Protestant Reformation, and to be many, one, and free; and (3) out of the Western tradition of secular republicanism, and to be many, one, and free. Indeed we may be seen to be, in a profounder sense than is usually meant, not just in the past but continuously, Out of Many—One. If that is what we are, or become, as a religious people under this Constitution, then we will indeed be what our Founders rather grandly claimed: a new order for the ages.

////Religion and the Constitution/////////////////////////////////
// Catherine L. Albanese, responder////

Serendipity ordained that, on the same day I was reading William Lee Miller's chapter on religion and the Constitution, I was also reading an American Antiquarian Society newsletter regarding a recent conference on the history of the book. There Michael Warner of Northwestern University, discussing the field of literature, outlined major directions in scholarship. Warner's brief historiographic tour culminated in a synopsis of the mid-twentieth-century New Criticism and then the New Historicism. In New Criticism what was important was the work in itself, with its own fixed and inherent meaning. Interpretation sought the universal, and it demanded study of the "narrative devices" that mediated the language of the text, its "thematic coherence," its "imagery patterns," and its "ironies and ambiguities."[1] By contrast, the New Historicism looked beyond the text to what we would call context, but it subsumed the context into the actual meaning of the text. In other words, the New Historicism saw culture not simply as background but as part of the text. Interpretations and values were up for grabs in the New Historicism, and the "politics of interpretation" ruled the day.[2]

---

[1]Michael Warner, "Literary Studies and the History of the Book," *The Book: Newsletter of the Program in the History of the Book in American Culture* 12 (July 1987): 3.

[2]Ibid., 4-5.

Something of the same two approaches is at work when we confront the text of one of the fundamental documents of our land, our Constitution. On the one hand, we can look at it as Warner's New Critics might, viewing it in terms of its own internal integrity, its textures of logical coherence and implicit meaning. We can read it as not so much marked by contact with a particular place and time or a particular cast of people and circumstances but as, in fact, universal in its import and value. On the other hand, like the advocates of the New Historicism, we can put the Constitution into a historical context, so that the beliefs and passions and actions of people past and present become part of the text of the document.

Miller, in some sense, does both in his own insightful text on the text. Directing keen attention to the document itself as he listens for the language of religion, he mostly discovers the silence around the Constitution's sounds. Yet, he hears in the silence the echoes of circumstantial evidence that tell about the religious bent of the writers. They exempt Sundays when they count the days the president is allowed for casting a veto to a bill. They date their document "in the year of our Lord." This evidence is not much to go on, and it mostly corroborates the old anecdote recorded by the nineteenth-century chronicler Benjamin F. Morris: "After the convention had adjourned, Rev. Dr. Miller, a distinguished professor in Princeton College, met Alexander Hamilton in the streets of Philadelphia, and said, 'Mr. Hamilton, we are greatly grieved that the Constitution has no recognition of God or the Christian religion.' 'I declare,' said Hamilton, 'we forgot it!' "[3]

The sounds of silence are suggestive in still another way when Miller addresses the question of the ideas—the implicit meanings—that ground the language of the Constitution. Its worldview, or religious philosophy of life, reflects the Calvinist Christianity that was dominant along the Atlantic seaboard. Its "hearty Puritanism" shapes its theory of checks and balances that, without saying so, acknowledges the doctrine of original sin. And likewise the Puritan strand in the nation's heritage

---

[3]In Benjamin F. Morris, *Christian Life and Character of the Civil Institutions of the United States* (Philadelphia: George W. Childs, 1864) 248.

shapes the sense of ''common-wealth'' the document reveals. ''We the people'' are autonomous beings, with powers to grant over to a government for the common good and other powers to retain. Covenant theology and the empowering freedom of the Word of God hover in the constitutional wings.

In light of this interpretation, Miller deserves an enthusiastic reception among the ranks of the New Critics. He has successfully analyzed a text and enabled it to yield important clues to its religious ambience. He has shown us its fabric of religious integrity and commitment. And he has found the key to its pattern of imaging and its thematic coherence, even as his subtle exposure of the dialectic between its Enlightenment faith and its Protestantism invites us to explore its ironies and ambiguities.

But if Miller is a faithful New Critic, he has also proved that he is, even more, a faithful New Historicist. Already in his detective work on the document he takes us behind and beyond the Constitution. And he does so still further to treat of religious movements that shaped its past and its continuing presence. Significantly, he points to the role of the First Amendment, with its establishment and free exercise clauses, in the development of the nation's distinctive form of religious pluralism.

Thus, as Miller follows the trajectory of the Constitution in American life, the context he brings to the text is not limited to the distant or immediate past that shaped the document. The context, instead, extends through American history on into our own times. In point of fact, he is telling us that the Constitution is alive. What it says is mediated by each new generation of American actors. What it says, it follows, is always either changing or open to change.

To sum up so far, Miller as New Critic examines the implicit and explicit meanings of the text of the Constitution as that text bears on the domain of religion. And Miller as New Historicist takes us outside the text to the forces that shaped it and continue still to shape its meaning. In so doing, he moves us toward a consideration of how the Constitution affects organized religion through its establishment and free exercise clauses.

All this is to the good. At the same time, there is still another way that we might act as New Historicists, expanding the scope of Miller's argument regarding religion and the Constitution.

It is surely a truism that religion is about belief. What we often forget, though (as sometimes the founders of the nation did), is that real religion, live religion, is also about behavior. Religion is not simply religious "opinion," an epiphenomenal crust that forms on the surface of the significant substance of life. It *is* the significance and the substance if it is alive and well. And so it follows that real religions are never simply belief systems. They are always action systems too. The Constitution recognized this fact in its First Amendment language of the free *exercise* of religion.

Even so, the Enlightenment climate of the Constitution's birth and the Protestant commitment that sustained it (as Miller has so well shown) combined to place the emphasis for later generations on religion as a system of beliefs. Any colonial Calvinist church, with its pulpit placed prominently in the sanctuary center, would have said as much. Any roving Gallup pollster who surveys the presence of religion in American life today by asking people if they *believe* in God and an afterlife is saying the same. However, if instead of stressing a view of religion as a system of beliefs we look at it mostly as an action system, a different—maybe richer—picture of the relationship between religion and the Constitution emerges.

First, in this action approach, we might consider the way the Constitution has functioned in American history as *itself* a religious object and center for a system of politics and government. We might see it as a powerful symbolic expression of the public religion that articulates the transcendent meaning we place on the nation.

To cite what is perhaps the most prominent eighteenth-century example, consider the great constitutional parade in Philadelphia, appropriately enough the "city of brotherly love." Here, on the Fourth of July in 1788, marching together in one division could be found "the clergy of the different Christian denominations, with the rabbi of the Jews, walking arm in arm." This organized "religious" division, however, was only one of some eighty-eight in the great parade. Marching in these other divisions were representatives of just about every trade and service offered by the new republic—house carpenters and saw makers, printers and bookbinders, sail makers and ship joiners, and on through a litany of labor. Borne along in the parade, too, were huge floats—patriotically inspired displays of the Constitution as the "new roof" or of the "federal ship Union," and more modest displays of "federal flour," a "federal printing press," and so forth.[4] Themes related to the federal Constitution were elaborated at far greater length and in far more intricate detail than I can recapture here, but I hope that I have said enough to suggest what, from a religious point of view, the iconography of the parade was proclaiming.

The celebrated "harmony" of Christian with Christian and Jew with Christian came because, as the structure of the parade told eloquently, Christians of whatever stripe, and Jews as well, had been assimilated into something higher—into the new public religion of the republic, with a sacred text in the Constitution.

Nor did the cultus of the Constitution die with the founding generation. Supreme Court justices, in the evolving doctrine of implied powers, looked to the constitutional "deposit of faith" to arrive at norms for living rightly in their own times. To pronounce a law unconstitutional was to mark it with a secular anathema, telling Americans, in so many words, that it was unscriptural. Indeed, the Supreme Court was swept into the constitutional cult so that, as Daniel Boorstin once remarked, it became "a kind of secular papacy" and the "Great Remembrancer of our foundations."[5] With the help of the Supreme Court and

---

[4]For a full account of the Philadelphia constitutional parade, see Francis Hopkinson, *Account of the Grand Federal Procession in Philadelphia, July 4, 1788, to Which Are Added Mr. Wilson's Oration, and a Letter on the Subject of the Procession* (Philadelphia: Carey, 1788) 1-14; and Benjamin Rush to Elias Boudinot [?], Philadelphia, 9 July 1788, in *Letters of Benjamin Rush*, ed. L. H. Butterfield, 2 vols. (Princeton: Princeton University Press, 1951) 1:470-75. For a treatment of the parade germane to my discussion here, see Catherine L. Albanese, *Sons of the Fathers: The Civil Religion of the American Revolution* (Philadelphia: Temple University Press, 1976) 212-16.

[5]Daniel J. Boorstin, in Robert McCloskey, *The American Supreme Court*, The Chicago History of American Civilization (Chicago: University of Chicago Press, 1960) v-vi.

its "remembrancing," therefore, Americans were able to blunt the rough edge of change by ascribing the newness of the present to the prescience of the past.

Meanwhile, at the center of the public religion, the Constitution functioned as a biblical icon. Certainly, the founding generation had been, for all intents and purposes, of that opinion.[6] And over the years, the document acquired more and more iconic power, as if the decades of community reverence began to inhere in the very parchment of the text. The Constitution went to New York in 1787 to join the Continental Congress, and later it was placed in the custody of the State Department. When the British invaded Washington during the War of 1812, the Constitution was spirited away from their path. In our own century, in 1924, it was moved to a special shrine in the Library of Congress, and the most visible acts of reverence began to be performed. Conditions for viewing the document were designed to prevent its physical deterioration, which had already by this time become noticeable. Then, in 1952, after a great public liturgy, a new shrine in the National Archives Building became the Constitution's resting place, side by side with the Declaration of Independence. Historian Dumas Malone called the shrine, not inappropriately, a sarcophagus.[7] And in a helium-filled case with special protective glass, the Constitution, with the Declaration, is summoned still to rise each day from its many-tonned vault of steel.

_____

[6]For example, Alexander Hamilton, who acknowledged that the Constitutional Convention had "forgotten" religion, also called the document a "prodigy." Philadelphia physician Benjamin Rush found it necessary to deny that the Constitution was explicitly "the offspring of inspiration." Later, James Madison was more forthright in linking it analogously with the Bible. Just as, in the Bible, the "cloudy medium" of language had made the divine communication "dim and doubtful," so the language of the great constitutional text had been unable to capture precisely the essence of the Framers' thinking. See Alexander Hamilton, "Federalist No. 85," in Alexander Hamilton, James Madison, and John Jay, *The Federalist,* ed. Benjamin F. Wright (Cambridge: Harvard University Press, 1961) 547; Benjamin Rush to Elias Boudinot [?], in *Letters of Benjamin Rush,* 1:475; James Madison, "Federalist No. 78," in Hamilton, Madison, and Jay, *Federalist,* 270.

[7]See Dumas Malone, *The Story of the Declaration of Independence* (New York: Oxford University Press, 1954) 264.

It is clear, therefore, that religious action in American public religion has meant ritual action to honor the Constitution. But if an action approach to religion can turn us inward, so to speak, to the history of ritual encounter with the Constitution's text, it can also turn us outward to the history of the encounter between that text and acting religious groups. Here the establishment, and especially, the free exercise clause beomes paramount. Here we meet the benefits of the Constitution's reigning idea that religion is equivalent to belief. William Miller has already spoken about the pluralism that the nation's fundamental law helped to foster, and we need only look around us in the late 1980s to assent to his assessment. Indeed, even for the eighteenth century new studies like Patricia Bonomi's *Under the Cope of Heaven* and Richard Pointer's *Protestant Pluralism and the New York Experience* are supplying a wealth of evidence about how plural American religion already was.[8]

Such religious proliferation was aided and abetted by understanding religion as belief. Because belief is, after all, about conjecture—and religious belief is about conjecture concerning what transcends, or goes beyond, the everyday world—it is, on its own, not nearly so powerful as action. By perceiving religion chiefly as belief, religious freedom could be guaranteed. Given the equality of all sects and religious opinions before the law, religion could never be construed as particularly dangerous to the commonweal.

But precisely here we encounter the limits of the Constitution's assumptions about religion. For if religion is, above all else, an action system, then we expect belief to engender behavior, and committed belief to express itself in strong and marked forms of action in the world. And when religious belief or opinion among some Americans becomes markedly different from the belief or opinion of most of their mainstream Protestant neighbors and fellow travelers, it follows that strange

---

[8]Patricia U. Bonomi, *Under the Cope of Heaven: Religion, Society, and Politics in Colonial America* (New York: Oxford University Press, 1986); and Richard Pointer, *Protestant Pluralism and the New York Experience* (Bloomington: Indiana University Press, in press).

and unusual (to their neighbors) forms of behavior may result. So it was, in the nineteenth century, that the new sect of Mormons scandalized other Americans and titillated untold numbers of newspaper audiences with their practice of polygamy. So it was, too, that during the same era Plains Indians frightened and shocked other Americans with their "barbaric superstition" in the Sun Dance, the Ghost Dance, and other such forms of ritual. And so it is, even in our own time, that small Appalachian mountain offshoots of Pentecostalism disturb the peace and sense of propriety of fellow Appalachians with the snake handling that forms the center of their ritual life.

In all these and similar instances, it is noteworthy that belief-become-behavior has earned, for these Americans, firm and unequivocal disapproval. The Constitution indeed guaranteed freedom of belief, but when it came to behavior—even behavior that affected mostly only members of the religious group in question—matters became more complicated. Questions of the morality of the community or the difference between religion and superstition or the demands of the public good became more important. The word made flesh proved itself a scandal to the nation.

To notice these facts of American history is not to denigrate the real achievement of the Constitution regarding the place of religion in relation to government. But it is to remind us that the picture is not so clean and tidy as we—or in the past, the Founders—might like it to be. And it is to remind us that the Founders, their conception of religion as normatively Christian and Protestant, and their enduring legacy of Christian/Protestant assumptions were deeply immersed in their time and place in history. For all of the universalism we like to see in the Constitution, the New Historicism reminds us of the Constitution's very particular roots and of its (as particular) history of interpretation. While in one sense the Constitution set the course, with splendid success, for a pluralistic nation, it did not possess the implicit framework, or the set of integrated meanings, that would enable its heirs to understand fully the religious situation it—and history—had spawned. The silence around the sounds of the Constitution when it came to religion was a *conceptual* silence. It would be challenged by the history of a nation with new peoples, new plans, and new religious preoccupations.

Given all of this, the true challenge of the present becomes the challenge to make the document work to accommodate and—more—support and buttress the evolving religious reality of the American nation. We have a new order of the ages to be sure, and the newness is a product not simply of the founding moment, new as that might have been. Still more, the newness is a product of the changes—including un-Protestant and un-Christian one—that history has made, and keeps on making, in the composition and plans and purposes of the American peoples.

////Religion and the Constitution//
// Sheldon Hackney, responder////

We have been getting a great deal of instruction lately on the Constitution, whose two-hundredth birthday we have been celebrating. Fireworks and grand federal processions capture our attention; historical snippets on television and daily reminders in the newspaper dole out knowledge by the thimbleful; scholarly tomes provide information and interpretation by the barrel; and Oliver North and Robert Bork in their different ways have provided real-life examples of the great document in action. We are happily awash in constitutional reverie.

In mid-September 1987, the *New York Times Magazine* published a special issue devoted to the Constitution. There were articles about the wonderful adaptability of the document, about minority groups and women, about states' rights and privacy and the commerce clause, but there was no article about religion. Now Professor Miller has told us why. Religion, *The First Freedom,* as Miller has previously written, is present in the Constitution primarily through exclusion and negation. But it is very much there, nonetheless.

The Constitution therefore should not be read as an antireligious document. Miller argues convincingly that the Revolution and the Constitution were the results of several different intellectual strands, but one of those was religious. The Constitution, then, can be seen as the culmination of religious principle, and it certainly must not be seen as the repudiation of religion. Miller comes close to arguing that the Constitution's ability to enshrine religious pluralism in our fundamental law was made possible by the existence in the eighteenth century of an assumed commonality in religion, one provided by Protestant Christianity. Because the Constitution freed the federal government of religious impediments, we were left free as a single people to be more religious than the European societies from which we had sprung. Irony and paradox are the stuff of interesting historical analysis.

One of the things we surely celebrate on this two-hundredth anniversary is the wisdom of the Founding Fathers in putting religion largely outside the realm of politics. As an issue of constitutional interpretation and strife, religion has been primarily a twentieth-century problem. It arose only after the Supreme Court began to apply the First Amendment to the states as a result of a new, more expansive view of the Fourteenth Amendment that began fifty years ago. That religion and politics do not mix very well is attested by the fact that we have just celebrated the twenty-fifth anniversary of the landmark school-prayer decision, and the issue is still very much alive with politicians, from the president on down.

Most successful politicians hate issues that polarize. They make life very uncertain and dangerous. Having to make a choice between two blocs of voters is risky business, so the prototypical political solution in the United States is for everyone to get a little piece of the pie. Spread it around. Keep everyone happy. The free-market version of this strategy is probably the most popular of all political responses to need: just put money in the hands of individuals and let them decide for themselves what they want. In this way, no enemies are made, because no choices are made.

This solution works very well when the good being sought is divisible: food, clothing, housing, entertainment, and individual consumption of all kinds. It does not work so well for those good things of life that do not lend themselves to being divided: clean air, clean water, police protection, or national defense. In those areas, each individual cannot simply be left to buy as much as he or she wants, while the neighbors buy whatever they want. Either everyone has it, or nobody has it.

Now, the problem arises for religion and morals when people think the thing under consideration is more like a common good than like an individual good. The Founding Fathers wisely wanted to put religious conflict outside the sphere of public life and public strife by saying that everyone should do his or her own thing and the government should not play favorites. We only have to look at the problems Israel has in trying to decide collectively what it means to be a Jewish state (which includes the question of what it means to be a Jew) to understand what anguish James Madison and his colleagues saved us from—at least until recently.

Pluralistic societies have a very difficult time deciding what moral values to enforce. Those are the most divisive issues because they cannot be compromised in the great American tradition of individual liberty. The abortion issue is a current example, and not only because it is morally complex. The proabortion forces couch their appeal in terms of free choice, a traditional American virtue. The antiabortion, or prolife, forces reply that it is morally repugnant to allow individual choice if one of the choices is murder. If one believes that eternal truth is on one's side, or that absolute standards of behavior are divinely sanctioned, the tolerance of deviation is immoral, sinful, and sacrilegious. Practicing politicians, therefore, would love to see the issue go away or be placed outside the bounds of politics in a definitive way by the Supreme Court.

We are brought back, then, to the central irony that is the theme of Miller's paper, the irony that is implied by our national motto, *e pluribus unum,* that the profound benefits and rewards of pluralism are to be realized only as we also recognize our commonality. How one may be different and what must be uniform, of course, is constantly in process of negotiation by a vigorous people, guided by the fundamental tenets set forth in the Constitution and Bill of Rights two hundred years ago.

Miller's paper is a charming and persuasive hymn in praise of the "benefits deriving from diversity within a people who are one." The religious part of this multipart chorus is an apt illustration of the dynamic tension between the centripetal and centrifugal forces in American life. We were "born free" as a nation, and thus we do not have to fight and refight all the historical battles of liberation from anachronistic political, social, and ecclesiastical forms; but we also miss those given forms, symbols, rituals, associations, and allegiances that help hold a society together. Because we are constantly in flux, buffeted by the up-rooting effects of migration across the continent, urbanization, indus-trialization, immigration, and rapid social change, we constantly feel that we are flying apart. We worry about what holds us together as a single people. The more pluralistic we become in the late twentieth cen-tury, the more problematic are the sources of unity and common pur-pose in American life.

Our multiplicity of religious loyalties tends to set us apart from each other, but our constitutionally ratified devotion to religious freedom can bind us together. Fashioning our increasingly diverse society into a just social order that respects differences *and* provides for equality contin-ues to be the most pressing task before us as a nation that trusts in God.

I think that Professor Miller's essay is excellent; it is fair, balanced, and illuminating. I see my remarks more as raising some hard questions that grow out of it than as offering any major disagreements with the paper itself. Since one of my areas of interest has been fundamentalism, I want to make some remarks on the implications of the paper for a favorite fundamentalist topic—what they call ''secular humanism.''

Miller alludes to one of the great problems facing our civilization today: Can we find a coherent public philosophy? This seems an especially vexing problem, as we have, first of all, a bewildering pluralism. Second, we have what Miller refers to as the problem of shallowness (shallowness, though, may actually temper the pluralism—Americans may be too shallow to fight about their differences). But third, within the last decades has emerged a particularly deep gulf between the ideological right and the ideological left that may be threatening whatever harmony there has been. This gap shows up in some issues over which there seem to be irreconcilable differences—such as abortion or over what is to be taught in the public schools. We see it in the furor over the Bork nomination.

Fundamentalists describe this split much too simplistically as one between Christians and secular humanists. In fact, there are Christians, secularists, and humanists on all sides of these issues. Nonetheless,

whatever we call it, there is a deep split that involves the strong influences of opponents of traditional religions on one side and strong influences of fundamentalist (and charismatic) Christians on the other.

Miller suggests some analogies between the situation today and the
divide between Christians and secularists in the eighteenth century. He
also proposes that we may be able to duplicate the eighteenth-century
solution to this problem. He suggests that, out of a synthesis of various
traditions, we may be able to blend a workable public philosophy. The
ethos that shaped the Constitution was a blend of classical, Christian,
British, and Enlightenment ideals. Out of one, many. I hope he is correct in this hope. I just want to reflect on some of the similarities and
differences in the situations in the two eras.

Though *secular humanism* is not the best term, it does refer to an iden-
tifiable worldview that has had immense influence on our civilization.
(Perhaps we could call it "nontheistic secularism," or "nontheistic natu-
ralism.") The premises of this worldview are that there is no God (or none
that we can know) and that the universe is the product solely of natural
causes. Values are therefore relative and derived from an evolutionary naturalistic framework. Usually such secularists hold that the world would be
better off without the absolute claims of traditional religions.

I think we could consider such philosophy, mutatis mutandi, as
roughly equivalent to eighteenth-century Enlightenment secularism, and
could agree that it should be treated constitutionally, more or less the
same way. Miller correctly points out that the Constitution certainly
protects such secularism.

The more problematic case is: What happens if the nontheists move
from being a sect to becoming the establishment? Here Miller also recognizes the danger and observes that, if the modern heirs to the Enlightenment "assume that their religionless outlook is *the* foundation of
America, that opinion needs to be challenged, too."

Here is indeed where the issue is being joined, and nowhere does
this constitutional question show up more clearly than in the nation's
public schools. As many have observed, the schools are the closest thing
we have to a religious establishment. Is there one coherent philosophy
that can be taught in public schools? Through most of our history we

have answered this question by some form of an assimilationist ideology. Miller is hopeful that we can continue to do so. Though such philosophies were far from representing the interests of everyone fairly (all sorts of minorities were discriminated against), they did at least represent a blend of a number of the most influential traditions.

Here, however, we get to the difference between the late eighteenth century and the late twentieth century. Most obviously, our social situation is more complex, we have more voices that have a legitimate claim to be heard, or at least not to be discriminated against. How can we say anything in a public philosophy that is not simply shallow? Anything substantive discriminates against some minority. So how can we have a comprehensive philosophy and a unified school system? Perhaps if we took our pluralism truly seriously, we would provide means so that at least part of our public education could be conducted under responsible pluralistic auspices.

This problem of social pluralism is related to a parallel problem of intellectual pluralism that separates us from the late eighteenth century. One of the reasons why the major competing philosophies in the American tradition could be assimilated into more-or-less workable synthesis was that all of these philosophies assumed fundamentally that truth is one, that there is one science, and that all rational people ought to be able to discover this truth. Protestant and Enlightenment thinkers (to take the most prominent examples) disagreed about how well the Bible fit their scientific standards; but they often could agree on just about everything else. Science, reason, and common sense, they all believed, were the same for the entire race, and so they did not need a special Protestant political science, or Protestant economics. All they needed was scientific learning to which one might or might not add Christian revelation.

Something like this set of assumptions prevailed until well into the twentieth century. It was challenged earlier, of course, but did not collapse until about the 1960s.

As long as most people shared the assumption that scientific truth is one, it did not create a huge problem for secularists if the American educational system was dominated by Protestants through the first century of the nation's history, and by the same token it did not create a huge problem for Protestants if their schools and universities were turned over to the secularists during the nation's second century. If truth was one, then we could all work together under the umbrella of disinterested learning, blending the insights from our various traditions and adding Bible courses and chapel attendance as options. One was not favoring any sect—so it was thought—if one simply taught the best science, social science, literary theory, or whatever of the day. So, out of many, we could get one.

Today, however, we face a far different intellectual situation. In brief, we face a rampant intellectual pluralism. Even regarding the hard sciences, it has been widely believed, since the advent of Thomas Kuhn, that scientific theories are community relative. Intellectual life is even more anarchical in other disciplines. Many are dominated by relativistic hermeneutical theories that in one way or another make the interpreter or the interpretive community sovereign. There is widespread denial that there is any way of adjudicating disputes among competing theories. Things are, of course, not as bad in practice as they are in theory. In fact, everyone has to live in the real world, and almost everyone acts as though they believe there still are some common standards. With many of the prevailing schools of thought so radically pluralist in principle, however, one wonders if there is really still much hope of bringing these competing ideologies together into a nice eighteenth-century blend.

One of the ironies of this situation is that it is the underlying philosophy identified with what I have called nontheistic secularism that has fostered this intellectual pluralism (which grows largely out of an evolutionary model in which ideas are a form of social adjustment). But at the same time that these nontheistic secularists are promoting such philosophies at the highest intellectual level, their communities are the most resistant to any challenges to a monolithic state-controlled public educational system. One wonders how they can have it both ways. If they claim that intellectual life is irredeemably pluralistic, then how can they claim that the underlying secularist or purely naturalistic assumptions of their worldview are simply based on "science" and that therefore a single essentially naturalistic and relativistic philosophy should control all self-respecting education?

The fundamentalists, to their credit, have successfully raised this issue. They have borrowed a page from the secularist philosophers in recognizing that there is not just one science, or just one social science, for all humanity—but that there are underlying worldviews, paradigms, systems of assumptions, or whatever, that dominate competing outlooks. In this respect the fundamentalists have faced the question of pluralism in America more squarely than have the nontheistic secularists. Unfortunately, fundamentalists have not understood well the theoretical bases for the issues they have raised. Actually they have operated more on the principle of appropriating whatever theory suits their self-interest. So they have ended up with badly confused and self-defeating approaches to these issues, such as proposing creation-science laws or objecting to the use of books such as *The Wizard of Oz* or *The Diary of Anne Frank*.

Nonetheless, however much we may deplore these tactics, I think we have to admit that fundamentalists are pointing to real issues concerning American pluralism and that their positions could be much more coherently defended. Partly because fundamentalists have too often spoken as though they actually wanted to reinstitute a Protestant establishment, too few people have taken seriously the legitimate issues concerning pluralism they *are* raising.

Perhaps it is still possible to come up with an assimilationist ideology that can please most major parties. But at least in public education, it seems to me that this solution is much more problematic than it was in the eighteenth century. It is certainly one of the unresolved issues on the constitutional agenda.

The Kingdom of God in America: Language of Faith, Language of Nation, Language of Empire

// Robert N. Bellah/////

Religion has played a central role in American public life from the first settlement to the present day. In this chapter I consider one highly significant way in which religion has influenced our public life: it has provided us with a public language, not only a language of faith, but a language of nation and even a language of empire. As we shall see, even our Constitution was interpreted religiously.

Some people, adopting a rather narrow and rather recent understanding of the First Amendment, would believe, or at least vaguely feel, that there is something illegitimate about the use of religion as a source of public language. They would be right if such language ever attained legally coercive authority, for of course that would involve the establishment of religion, prohibited by the First Amendment. But the use of religion in public discourse, in the noncoercive discussion that goes on between citizens, is not only not prohibited by the Constitution, it is specifically protected by it. That is one of the meanings of the ''free exercise'' clause of the First Amendment. But even though the use of religious language in public discourse is legitimate as such, it is not without its pitfalls. It is also a legitimate part of public discourse to consider when religious language, used to interpret our common problems, is helpful and when it may be dangerous, either to the faith community, to the national community, or to both. This chapter considers not the legitimacy but the appropriateness of the use of certain kinds of religious language in our common life.

Perry Miller has argued that John Winthrop's Sermon "A Model of Christian Charity," delivered on board ship in Salem Harbor in 1630 before the colonists had even landed, stands at the beginning of American consciousness.[1] At that moment Winthrop addressed the settlers as members of a church, though also as members about to establish a society, what Winthrop calls a "plantation," the Massachusetts Bay Colony. He enjoins the congregation in words almost entirely drawn from the New Testament:

> For this end, we must be knit together in this work as one man, we must entertain each other in brotherly affection, we must be willing to abridge ourselves of our superfluities, for the supply of others' necessities, we must uphold a familiar commerce together in all meekness, gentleness, patience and liberality, we must delight in each other, make others' conditions our own, rejoice together, mourn together, labor and suffer together, always having before our eyes our commission and community in the work, our community as members of the same body.

Then, as he draws toward his conclusion, he says,

> For we must consider that we shall be as a city upon a hill, the eyes of all people are upon us; so that if we shall deal falsely with our God in this work we have undertaken and so cause him to withdraw his present help from us, we shall shame the faces of many of God's worthy servants, and cause their prayers to be turned into curses upon us till we be consumed out of the good land whither we are going.[2]

---

[1]Perry Miller, *Nature's Nation* (Cambridge: Harvard University Press, 1967) 6.

[2]John Winthrop, "A Model of Christian Charity," in *Puritan Political Ideas,* ed. by Edmund S. Morgan, 92-93. I have modernized the spelling.

The image of the city on a hill comes, of course, from Matthew 5:14, early in the Sermon on the Mount, where Jesus says, "Ye are the light of the world. A city that is set on an hill cannot be hid," and it serves as one of several metaphors for the kingdom of God. Winthrop then closes his sermon with a quotation from Moses' last farewell to Israel, Deuteronomy 30, thus bringing in the Exodus and covenant imagery, which is the primary locus of the kingdom of God idea in the Hebrew Scriptures.

H. Richard Niebuhr has argued that the kingdom of God is the master symbol of American Christianity,[3] though he did not comment on this sermon of John Winthrop. It is certainly a complex symbol, both in Scripture and in Winthrop. The idea of kingdom could not but be political, and in its New Testament usage it pointed back not only to Moses but to the great days of David and Solomon. By endowing Jesus with a Davidic lineage, the New Testament certainly alluded to that meaning, yet by showing a Jesus crowned as "king of the Jews" only while dying the death of a political criminal on the cross, it showed that the kingdom of God must certainly have meaning other than worldly power. Jesus proclaimed that the kingdom of God was at hand, so that it was actually taking shape in the beloved community of those who took up their cross and followed him. Yet, it was also said to be still to come, to be fully realized only when Jesus comes again. And even for those who participate in it now, there is something conditional about it. In the passage just before the mention of the city on the hill, Jesus says, using another metaphor for the kingdom, "Ye are the salt of the earth: but if the salt have lost his savour, wherewith shall it be salted?" (Matt. 5:13).

When Winthrop said, "We shall be as a city upon a hill," he was certainly using the language of faith, but he was also incipiently using the language of nation, for it was not just the church of Jesus Christ but the plantation of New England that Winthrop was referring to. When Ronald Reagan quotes Winthrop, as he did at the July 4 Statue of Liberty celebration in 1986, but frequently elsewhere as well, he embel-

---

[3]H. Richard Niebuhr, *The Kingdom of God in America* (New York: Harper and Brothers, 1937).

lishes both Winthrop and the New Testament by saying that the Americans have a mission to be "a *shining* city upon a hill." We may wonder whether he is not extending the metaphor still further to refer to the American empire in all its wealth and power, thus adding a language of empire to the languages of faith and nation. Winthrop retained a strong sense of the conditional meaning of the image of a city upon a hill, reminding us that if we are unfaithful we may be consumed out of this good land. With Reagan the element of warning seems to be largely subsumed in the rhetoric of celebration.

Already in the seventeenth century Roger Williams worried about extending the language of faith into a language of nation. He would have been amazed indeed to see that language become a language of empire. He admonished Winthrop and his colleagues not to identify Massachusetts with the kingdom of God, since "America (as Europe and all nations) lies dead in sin."[4] His warning was frequently reiterated but not frequently heeded in our subsequent history.

It was perhaps inevitable that the colonists, particularly the pious among them, would see themselves under the archetype of the Exodus. Cotton Mather in his biography of Winthrop refers to him as Moses, because he led his people across the sea to a promised land.[5] As Perry Miller has pointed out, the biblical image of the "errand into the wilderness" was powerfully present among the New England settlers.[6] It is therefore worth remembering that the Hebrew conception of the kingdom of God was most clearly articulated at Sinai. God replaced Pharaoh as the king of kings; from then on, all earthly rulers were deprived of ultimate authority. Certainly the colonists saw themselves as escaping from the thrall of European empire to establish a new society under God in the wilder-

---

[4]Quoted in Sacvan Bercovitch, *The Puritan Origins of the American Self* (New Haven: Yale University Press, 1975) 110. I have modernized the spelling.

[5]Mather's life of Winthrop is conveniently reprinted as an appendix to Bercovitch, *Puritan Origins.*

[6]Perry Miller, *Errand into the Wilderness* (Cambridge: Harvard University Press, 1956).

ness. As such, the Exodus symbolism had for them the same meaning that liberation theologians have given it in the contemporary third world.

Yet, there was a troubling element in the Exodus symbolism that unfortunately had powerful social consequences. New England, like ancient Canaan, was not empty. It was all too easy for the colonists to identify the native Americans with the Amalekites, Jebusites, and Canaanites that God in the Hebrew Scriptures had ordered the children of Israel to replace. It is one of the ironies of that complex story that the Hebrews, in escaping from the imperial tyranny of one people, should inflict something similar on others. Again it was Roger Williams, almost alone, who protested against that analogy, arguing that the settlers had no right to take the land of others by force and that the American Indians were as much children of God as the English. The New England effort to build a "peaceable kingdom" (another synonym for the kingdom of God) has stood as a paradigm for the American experiment as a whole. It is in many ways an inspiring example, but also one deeply flawed. We need to remember both aspects.

Exodus imagery was by no means limited to the seventeenth century. It has reverberated throughout our history, in part because America has been the promised land for many diverse groups who have crossed many different seas to reach these shores, right up to the present. But the period of the Revolution and the Constitution of the new republic saw a particularly vigorous recrudescence of it. Nicholas Street, for example, preached a sermon in East Haven, Connecticut, in April 1777, entitled "The American States Acting Over the Part of the Children of Israel in the Wilderness and Thereby Impeding Their Entrance into Canaan's Rest."[7] He told his fellow citizens that it was not enough for them to have escaped from Pharaoh's oppressions. They must now come to terms with their own wickedness, rather than fall into backsliding and complaining, if they are to establish themselves securely in the promised land.

---

[7]In *God's New Israel: Religious Interpretations of American Destiny*, ed. by Conrad Cherry (Englewood Cliffs NJ: Prentice-Hall, 1971) 67-81.

For our purposes, an even more interesting sermon is one preached by Samuel Langdon to the General Court at Concord, New Hampshire, on 5 June 1788, entitled "The Republic of the Israelites an Example to the American States." Langdon was urging that New Hampshire become the ninth state to ratify the new federal Constitution and thus put it into effect, an outcome that occurred on 21 June. Langdon took as his text a passage from a speech of Moses: "Behold, I have taught you statutes and judgments, even as the Lord my God commanded me, that ye should do so in the land whither ye go to possess it. Keep therefore and do them; for this is your wisdom and your understanding in the sight of the nations, which shall hear all these statutes, and say, Surely this great nation is a wise and understanding people" (Deut. 4:5-6).[8] Langdon was not being entirely anachronistic when he argued that the government that God established at Sinai was republican in form. Recent biblical scholarship has confirmed that the Sinaitic covenant did establish a government that was significantly more egalitarian than the imperial models that it replaced. Part of the meaning of the "kingdom of God" there established was its new more egalitarian form. Langdon said, "If I am not mistaken, instead of the twelve tribes of Israel, we may substitute the thirteen states of the American Union," and proceeded to argue that "God in the course of his kind providence hath given you an excellent constitution of government, founded on the most rational, equitable, and liberal principles," which therefore deserves ratification.[9]

Later still, Lyman Beecher, stalwart leader of Connecticut Congregationalism, declared, "Our own republic in its Constitution and laws is of heavenly origin. It was not borrowed from Greece or Rome, but from the Bible. . . . It was God that gave these elementary principles to our forefathers, as the 'pillar of fire by night, and the cloud by day,' for their guidance."[10] But Exodus imagery is not the only indication of the centrality of the conception of the kingdom of God at the time of the

---

[8]Ibid., 93.

[9]Ibid., 98.

[10]Quoted in Niebuhr, *Kingdom of God*, 174.

birth of the republic. Ruth Bloch has shown in great detail the extraordinary resurgence of millennial themes at the time of the Revolution, and even into the 1790s, that saw the new nation as inextricably involved with the coming of the kingdom of God in the fullness of times.[11]

H. Richard Niebuhr, in an influential article entitled "The Idea of Covenant and American Democracy,"[12] has pointed out that biblical ideas of covenant competed with Enlightenment conceptions of contract as basic understandings of the new nation. The contractarian view sees individuals as entering a social contract to establish a government of fair procedures in order that they can maximize their self-interests. Robin Lovin has recently described the contrasting view.

> A covenant society is one in which the members are bound together by choice, by mutual commitment, more than by chance. A covenant society is one in which the members see their moral obligations as growing out of this commitment, so that they not only hold their neighbors to a higher ethical standard of conduct than they might if they were just thrown together at random; they expect more of themselves and they acknowledge that others who share in the covenant have a right to examine and criticize their behavior. Above all, the covenant creates this sense of mutual accountability not only to one another, but before God. It is not the moral health of each individual which is under scrutiny, but the righteousness or waywardness of the whole society. This sense that there is a common good, a well-being of the whole society that cannot be measured just by summing up the achievements and faults of all the individuals in it, is crucial to the covenant idea.[13]

Niebuhr argued that it was such ideas as these, rooted in an idea of covenant derived from the covenant at Sinai, still vividly in the minds of

---

[11]Ruth Bloch, *Visionary Republic: Millennial Themes in American Thought, 1756–1800* (Cambridge: Cambridge University Press, 1985).

[12]H. Richard Niebuhr, "The Idea of Covenant and American Democracy," *Church History* 23 (1954): 126-35.

[13]Robin W. Lovin, "Social Contract or a Public Covenant?" in *Religion and American Public Life*, ed. Robin W. Lovin 135.

the citizens of the new republic, that enriched our understanding of the new nation and laid the basis for a conception of democracy as a genuine quest for the common good, not merely a convenient contract for the pursuit of private goods.

It is interesting that, in the early days of the republic, the emergence of a language of empire came from the contractarian rather than the covenantal view of society. It was not millenarians but those pressing for the legitimacy of individual economic interests who began to speak of America's becoming "a whole empire," one that "may be extended farther and farther to the utmost ends of the earth."[14] However, the belief in the unbounded possibility of economic and scientific progress, which sometimes joined with dreams of empire, can be interpreted as a secular form of millennialism.

Not all secularists, however, were proponents of empire. Thomas Jefferson came as close to being a pacifist president as we have ever had. He shared the republican suspicion of military establishments and foreign wars as invitations to tyranny. He met British and French interference with our foreign trade with embargoes rather than armaments. It was through no fault of his that the largest accession of territory ever gained by the United States, the Louisiana Purchase, occurred during his presidency. Jefferson had sought to buy only New Orleans as an outlet for American trade on the Mississippi River. It was really the heroic resistance of the slave revolt in Haiti led by Toussaint Louverture that made Napoleon give up his plans for an empire in the New World and offer to sell the whole Louisiana Territory. Americans have never recognized how much they owe to the Haitians for this bloodless acquisition.[15]

Nonetheless, under Jefferson's successor, Madison, America undertook a war, the War of 1812, whose purposes were far from clear, but the motivation for which, at least in the war faction of the Republican party, was imperial. Indeed, it could be said that the war was fought

---

[14]Quoted in Cathy Matson and Peter Onuf, "Toward a Republican Empire: Interest and Ideology in Revolutionary America," *American Quarterly* 37 (1985): 516.

[15]Henry Adams, *History of the United States during the First Administration of Thomas Jefferson,* Library of America (1986 [1889]) vol. 1, chap. 15.

for two ends: Canada and Florida. The New England clergy, reflecting perhaps the opposition to the war on secular grounds by many of their parishioners, nevertheless added a principled opposition on the grounds that a war to gain territory by force is never justified.[16] It would seem that neither the orthodox language of faith nor the Jeffersonian language of nation gave much support to the imperial aspirations that were so thoroughly balked at, at the end of the War of 1812, when we were lucky to be able to return to the borders we had had at its beginning. But neither were the dreams of empire, which had, after all, long predated the War of 1812, subjected to searching criticism. The New England clergy did not, as far as I know, turn to 1 Samuel 8 to see whether the Americans were not in danger of making the same mistake as the ancient Hebrews—namely, abandoning their covenant heritage in order to imitate the great empires around them.

The Mexican-American War of 1845 raised again the question of empire and called out a complex of responses that would be well worth analysis, although the issues were still far from clear. It is in situations of war that issues of national survival, extension of empire, and the incompatibility of violence and faith come to intense public scrutiny. While elements of empire had been present in the American experience from the first forcible acquisition of Indian land, it was not till the very end of the nineteenth century, at the time of the Spanish-American War, that faith, nation, and empire seemed to flow together in a new synthesis, not without challenge, but enormously attractive to many of our citizens.

The religious response to imperialism was prepared by a growing identification of Protestant millennialism and secular ideas of progress, including the then-popular ideas about the role of race in history. Even among supporters of the Social Gospel, Anglo-Saxon superiority was taken for granted. Josiah Strong, a reforming clergyman, in his enormously popular book *Our Country,* published in 1885, developed a conception of racial progress that was more cultural than biological, but was still stunning in its implications:

---

[16]Henry Adams, *History of the United States during the Second Administration of James Madison,* Library of America (1986 [1891]) vol. 2, chap. 1.

The unoccupied arable lands of the earth are limited and will soon be taken. . . . Then will the world enter into a new stage of its history— *the final competition of races, for which the Anglo-Saxon is being schooled.* . . . Then this race of unequaled energy, with all the majesty of numbers and the might of wealth behind it— the representative, let us hope, of the largest liberty, the purest Christianity, the highest civilization—having developed peculiarly aggressive traits calculated to impress its institutions upon mankind will spread itself over the earth. . . . Can anyone doubt that the result of this competition of races will be the "survival of the fittest"? . . . Nothing can save the inferior race but a ready and pliant submission. . . . The contest is not one of arms, but of vitality and civilization.[17]

But when, in 1898 in the war with Spain, it did come to a contest of arms, the Protestant clergy on the whole did not flinch. The Presbyterian *Interior* heard in the war "the ringing of the bell of Divine Providence calling those who have the gospel of the world's salvation to see and to seize this new, this august opportunity for preaching it in a world-empire that has so long been waiting for it." The Baptist *Standard* published articles on the "imperialism of righteousness."[18] But it was the irrepressible Sen. Albert J. Beveridge who outdid even Josiah Strong in the fusion of social-Darwinist racism with religion: "The American Republic is a part of the movement of a race—the most masterful race of history—and race movements are not to be stayed by the hand of man. They are mighty answers to Divine commands. Their leaders are not only statesmen of peoples—they are prophets of God."[19]

Catholic prelates were somewhat more restrained in their celebration of this war with a Catholic nation, but their sentiments were not very different in the end. Through the war Archbishop John Ireland saw God's assigning "to this republic the mission of putting before the world

---

[17]In *Nationalism and Religion in America,* ed. Winthrop S. Hudson (New York: Harper and Row, 1970) 115.

[18]Quoted in Martin E. Marty, *Modern American Religion,* vol. 1, *The Irony of It All, 1893–1919* (Chicago: University of Chicago Press, 1987) 308.

[19]Quoted in ibid., 310.

the ideal of popular liberty, the ideal of the high elevation of all humanity.''[20] Protestants and Catholics alike seemed to be prepared to believe that America ''can conquer but to save.'' Nor was there an essentially different understanding among secular progressives who identified the nation with democracy, science, and progress.

Woodrow Wilson articulated a public philosophy with strong overtones of Protestant millennialism in leading America into World War I as a crusade to make the world safe for democracy, and men like John Dewey and Herbert Croly, who hardly shared his religious enthusiasm, were glad to join him on secular grounds. Yet, it was the profound disillusionment brought on by World War I and its aftermath that gave widespread expression to doubts that had been building as to the validity of the fusion of faith, nation, and empire. I would like to dwell for a moment on two of the critical precursors because they both used the symbolism of the kingdom of God to undercut the prevailing consensus.

American Protestants, as we have seen, had long been fascinated with the millennium, the coming kingdom of God. The decades before World War I had seen a hardening of the distinction between two views: *postmillennialism,* which saw Christ coming at the end of the millennium, and *premillennialism,* which saw him as coming, after catastrophic disruptions, at its beginning. Postmillennialism was the natural position of the liberals, for whom the achievements of secular culture were the gradual preparation for the millennial age. Premillennialism was growing among those who were increasingly disillusioned by those secular achievements and whose only hope for the future was direct divine intervention. Those who expected an imminent apocalypse hoped to limit their relation to the principalities and powers of this world and live in accordance with the teachings of Jesus. Such views led many of them to a pacifist position of opposition to the war and to American involvement in it. In 1915, *The King's Business,* the leading premillennial magazine, held that for God there is '' 'neither Greek nor Jew,' . . . English, German, or American.'' The editors, therefore, held that ''we must never forget we are brethren, and we must show our love for one

---

[20]Quoted in ibid., 307.

another in every way possible. . . . 'Vengeance' belongs to God, not to us. . . . Our part is to feed our hungry enemy (Rom. XII:20) and to 'overcome evil with good.' "[21]

In 1917, leading liberal theologians, particularly at the University of Chicago, began an unrestrained attack on the premillennialists for undermining patriotism and threatening national security. Professor Shirley Jackson Case of Chicago charged that money to support the pre-millennialists was coming from German sources. "The American nation," he argued, "is engaged in a gigantic effort to make the world safe for democracy." Therefore, "it would be almost traitorous negligence to ignore the detrimental character of premillennial propaganda. . . . In the name of religion we are told that the world cannot appreciably be improved by human efforts."[22] That the premillennialists not long after, under enormous pressure, largely abandoned their opposition to the war does not change the emblematic nature of the moment when they put the language of faith above the language of nation and empire. Nor can we fail to be instructed by the hysteria with which a liberal theologian defended his identification of Christianity with the American mission to make the world safe for democracy.

My second example is the Harvard philosopher Josiah Royce, who, though a member of no church, developed a remarkable philosophy of community on the basis of New Testament teachings. In his most important book, *The Problem of Christianity,* published in 1913, he took the "Kingdom of Heaven" as proclaimed by Jesus in the Sermon on the Mount as the beginning of a community whose meaning has only gradually unfolded.[23] Royce attributed extraordinary importance to Paul as the one who understood that Jesus' proclamation of the kingdom of heaven meant the creation of a community that would ultimately be uni-

---

[21]Quoted in George Marsden, *Fundamentalism and American Culture: The Shaping of Twentieth-Century Evangelicalism, 1870–1925* (New York: Oxford University Press, 1980) 144-45.

[22]Quoted in ibid., 146-47.

[23]Josiah Royce, *The Problem of Christianity* (Chicago: University of Chicago Press, 1968 [1913]) 135-36 and passim.

versal. For Royce the "detached individual" outside any community is lost, but any community, such as the nation, that would absolutize itself, would express only another form of "the individualism of the detached individual." He argued that the life of community, so essential for the moral and spiritual life of human beings, can be realized finally only in the "great community" that includes the entire human race.[24]

It is interesting in this connection to see Royce speaking out already in 1905 in his essay "Race Questions and Prejudices," opposing the "scientific" racism so prominent in his day and defending the dignity of Asians and blacks. He concludes the essay by writing, "For my part, then, I am a member of the human race, and this is a race which is, as a whole, considerably lower than the angels, so that the whole of it very badly needs race-elevation. In this need of my race I personally and very deeply share. And it is in this spirit only that I am able to approach our problem."[25]

Royce was appalled by World War I and, like the premillennialists, tried for awhile to stay above the struggle. After the sinking of the *Lusitania,* on which several of his friends and former students were lost, he came to identify the Allied cause with the cause of humanity, in spite of his deep attachment to German culture. His family and friends believed that the anguish the war caused him hastened his death, in 1916.[26]

Henry May has argued that, by the end of World War I, the near establishment of what he has characterized as Progressive Patriotic Protestantism came to an end, unable to cope with the collapse of its worldview that the war brought about.[27] Certainly the Protestant hege-

---

[24]Josiah Royce, "The Hope of the Great Community" [1916], in *The Basic Writings of Josiah Royce,* 2 vols. (Chicago: University of Chicago Press, 1969) 2:1145-63.

[25]Josiah Royce, "Race Questions and Prejudices" [1905], in *Basic Writings,* 2:1089-1110.

[26]John Clendenning, *The Life and Thought of Josiah Royce* (Wisconsin, 1985) chap. 10.

[27]Henry F. May, *Ideas, Faiths, and Feelings: Essays on American Intellectual and Religious History, 1952–1982* (New York: Oxford University Press, 1983) 171-72. Chapter 9 of this book, "The Religion of the Republic," was suggestive in my reflections for the present paper.

mony in American culture has been broken, and religious communities, Protestant included, have become more skeptical of identifying national and religious commitments. Yet, not only have religious groups continued to be active in our public life, religious language has continued to provide a source for public discussion. I conclude by considering two books by H. Richard and Reinhold Niebuhr that have clarified our understanding in this area and two pastoral letters of the American Catholic bishops that are exemplary of current practice.

In 1937, H. Richard Niebuhr published a book, *The Kingdom of God in America,* whose title I have chosen for this chapter. This book is an effort to determine the genuine religious impulse of American Christianity and to distinguish it, as far as possible, from the cultural or social use of religion for nonreligious ends. Niebuhr distinguishes three aspects of the kingdom on which American Protestants have focused successively in the seventeenth, eighteenth, and nineteenth centuries: divine sovereignty, reign of Christ, and coming kingdom. We have seen examples of all three aspects already in this paper. Rather than rehearse his argument, I would like to develop its implications for the appropriate and inappropriate use of religious language in public life.

The sovereignty of God is a central tenet of biblical teaching made indelible in the consciousness of Jews and Christians in the events of the Exodus and covenant at Sinai. Niebuhr characterizes it as it was understood by the early colonists:

> These early American Protestants believed in the kingdom of God, but it was not a society of peace and concord to be established by men of good will; it was rather the living reality of God's present rule, not only in human spirits but also in the world of nature and of human history. His kingdom was not an ideal dependent for its realization on human effort; men and their efforts were dependent upon it; loyalty to it and obedience to its laws were the conditions of their temporal and eternal welfare.[28]

---

[28]Niebuhr, *Kingdom of God,* 51.

With such a God it was possible for human beings to enter a covenant relationship if they accepted his sovereignty and the obligations that
flowed from it. The religious community was understood as founded on
just such a covenant relationship. The idea of a covenant society gen-
eralized beyond the church to the understanding of civil society undoubtedly lies behind some of the noblest achievements of the American
experiment. But it was subject to a subtle perversion. Niebuhr describes
the danger well:

> The old idea of American Christians as a chosen people who had been
> called to a special task was turned into the notion of a chosen nation
> especially favored. . . . As the nineteenth century went on the note of
> divine favoritism was increasingly sounded. Christianity, democracy,
> Americanism, the English language and culture, the growth of industry
> and science, American institutions—these are all confounded and con-
> fused. The contemplation of their own righteousness filled Americans
> with such lofty and enthusiastic sentiments that they readily identified
> it with the righteousness of God. . . . Henceforth the kingdom of the
> Lord was a human possession, not a permanent revolution. It is in par-
> ticular the kingdom of the Anglo-Saxon race, which is destined to bring
> light to the gentiles by means of lamps manufactured in America. Thus
> institutionalism and imperialism, ecclesiastical and political, go hand
> in hand.[29]

The idea of the reign of Christ is rooted in the proclamation of Jesus
that the kingdom is at hand and has come into being with his presence
in the world. Niebuhr sees the reign of Christ as experienced above all
as the fruit of repentance.

> The kingdom of Christ was the rule of sincerity in lives which had been
> made to understand the deviousness and trickery of the well loved ego
> as it skulks and hides in the labyrinthine ways of the mind, and which,
> having been made to see that they lived by forgiveness and not merit,
> needed no longer to defend themselves against themselves, their fellow
> men and God. The kingdom of Christ was the liberty of those who had

---

[29]Ibid., 179.

received some knowledge of the goodness of God and who reflected in their lives the measure of their knowledge and devotion.[30]

Since the beloved community that actualizes the reign of Christ sees itself as founded on the self-giving of God in Jesus Christ, it is called to a life of neighbor love without limit. Out of such an understanding many of the humanitarian impulses of nineteenth-century America had their origin, notably the antislavery movement. Nonetheless, as with the idea of the sovereignty of God, the idea of the reign of Christ was subject to perversion if it gave rise to self-righteousness. A particularly dangerous temptation was intoxication with the goodness of the end, so that one forgets the quality of the means. Even in so noble a cause as opposition to slavery, for the Christian, resort to violence is a catastrophic failure. For Niebuhr, as for Lincoln, the Civil War stands as a stern judgment on a nation that believed itself to be Christian but did not know how to solve its gravest problem by the application of the teachings of Christ.

The third aspect of the kingdom of God that Niebuhr singles out is the coming kingdom, the focus on the millennium, which we have seen has been so powerful in America. This great idea has been associated with some of the noblest impulses of Americans but also has its characteristic distortions. Where it has become literalistic, it has gotten bogged down in complex theories and numerical calculations. The temptation to self-righteousness, the characteristic American perversion, can appear when there is too quick an identification of the coming kingdom with the American project. Such a temptation is most effectively opposed when the coming kingdom is seen as judgment as well as consummation. Theodore Weld, the great antislavery evangelist, reminded his fellow citizens that millennial hope cannot be separated from the day of wrath, when he said,

> The land is full of blood. . . . The poor have cried and ears have been stopped and hearts have been steeled; and avarice has clutched the last pittance, and lust has gored itself with spoil, and prejudice has spurned God's image with loathing, and passion has rushed upon the helpless

---

[30]Ibid., 105.

and trodden down the needy in the gate; and when iniquity has been visited by terrible rebuke, it has swelled with pride and gnashed with rage, and cursed the poor and blasphemed God—scorning repentance and defying wrath to the uttermost. . . . What can save us as a nation but repentance—immediate, profound, *public,* proclaimed abroad, wide as our infamy and damning guilt have gone![31]

It was particularly easy for American liberals to forget the elements of judgment and repentance and to imagine that the kingdom would come in America smoothly and inevitably. Niebuhr gives his incisive characterization:

> The idea of the coming kingdom was robbed of its dialectical element. It was all fulfillment of promise without judgment. . . . In its one-sided view of progress which saw the growth of the wheat but not the tares, the gathering of the grain but not the burning of the chaff, this liberalism was indeed naively optimistic.
>
> A God without wrath brought men without sin into a kingdom without judgment through the ministrations of a Christ without a cross.[32]

Thus in 1937, H. Richard Niebuhr completed his survey of the Christian vision as applied to American life and assessed its strengths as well as its distortions. We can apply his insights to our present situation with the help of his brother Reinhold, who published in 1952, at the height of the cold war, a book that advances the insights of *The Kingdom of God in America* an important step forward. H. Richard saw the central tension between the community of faith and the nation, and he argued that the language of faith had to be true to itself if it was to provide genuine insight to the nation. To translate the language of faith into the language of the nation by eliminating religious transcendence was for him not only a total failure to understand the idea of the kingdom of God in any of its aspects but a prelude to disaster. He saw the problem of empire, but it was not central to his argument.

----

[31]Quoted in ibid., 159.

[32]Ibid., 193.

By 1952, America had become, almost overnight, the head of the greatest empire the world had ever known, and one locked in a cold war with another empire of lesser although immense power. Consequently, the scope of Reinhold's *The Irony of American History* is much more global than that of *The Kingdom of God in America*. In many ways the book is a product of its time, one-sided in its views, and expressing a brittle anti-Communism that seems paranoid today. It is thus all the more remarkable that Reinhold Niebuhr produced a book that is a profound critique of America and a severe warning to America at the peak of empire. By "irony" he means to point out the deep connection between our achievements and our failures, to which we remain blind as long as we do not see ourselves as sinners, something that Americans, whether they go to church or not, are loath to do. Far from an assertion of American virtue, *The Irony of American History* is a call for repentance:

> We cannot expect even the wisest of nations to escape every peril of moral and spiritual complacency; for nations have always been constitutionally self-righteous. But it will make a difference whether the culture in which the policies of nations are formed is only as deep and as high as the nations's ideals; or whether there is a dimension in the culture from the standpoint of which the element of vanity in all human ambitions and achievements is discerned. But this is a height which can be grasped only by faith. . . . The God before whom "the nations are as a drop in the bucket and are counted as small dust in the balances" is known by faith and not by reason. . . . The faith which appropriates the meaning in the mystery inevitably involves an experience of repentance for the false meanings which the pride of nations and cultures introduces into the pattern. Such repentance is the true source of charity; and we are more desperately in need of genuine charity than of more technocratic skills.[33]

In closing the book, even though he has excoriated the Communists, he reminds us that both sides are in need of contrition and that there is still the possibility of reaching out to the other side. Finally, he says that,

---

[33]Reinhold Niebuhr, *The Irony of American History* (New York: Scribner's, 1952) 149-50.

if we should perish, the primary cause would be not "the ruthlessness
of the foe" but "that the strength of a giant nation was directed by eyes
too blind to see all the hazards of the struggle; and the blindness would
be induced not by some accident of nature or history but by hatred and
vainglory."[34] Indeed, hatred and vainglory are the besetting sins of empire.

Today the empire, though still immensely powerful, is crumbling.
Our problems are enormous, at home and abroad. The naive optimism
and self-confidence that characterized us for so long is missing, and
nostalgically, many of us wish it to return. What are the lessons we can
learn from the ways in which Americans have used religious language,
particularly the language of the kingdom of God, to understand our
common problems?

Under the free exercise clause of the First Amendment, it is per-
fectly legitimate for the language of faith to operate as a public language
in America. It is of vital importance that we use the language of faith to
reflect on the problems of nation and empire—only in that way can the
members of faith communities bring their deepest insights to public attention. But it is a doubtful and dangerous enterprise to use the language
of faith as a language of nation and certainly as a language of empire.
To see the nation as a community that has entered a covenant to pursue
the good in common, with all participating, and to care especially for
those most in need, is admirable. But insofar as the nation is based on
coercion and coercion is not part of the kingdom of God, then the language of faith applied to the nation must always be analogical, not lit-
eral. And as far as we use it at all in our civic life, we must be committed,
as was Martin Luther King, Jr., to the use of nonviolence. It is a more
normal function of the community of faith to call the nation to repentance than to congratulate it on its righteousness.

With respect to empire the tension grows more acute. Jews and
Christians have had a long history of misfortune at the hands of empire.
That God's new Israel has become the world's most powerful empire is
a truth so chilling that most Americans, religious or not, would rather

---

[34]Ibid., 174.

not think about it.[35] Some of us know, and others of us would rather not know, that the Contras in Nicaragua are fighting not for democracy but for the control of Central America by the American empire. We were never bothered by dictators in Nicaragua as long as they were *our* dictators. We have heard those in high places use the language of faith to justify empire when they speak loosely of Armageddon, shining cities, and evil empires. But to do so is even more deeply troubling than to use the language of faith to justify a nation, for an empire rests on the coercion of other nations and its essence is vast military power. Of course, empires too exist under the sovereignty of God and may sometimes (ironically, Reinhold Niebuhr would say) work for good. Yet, if the nation requires judgment, then all the more does empire. Many speaking the language of faith today call for the creation of a new international order based on justice and participation to replace the division of the world into competing empires armed to the teeth. Reinhold Niebuhr would remind us to be realistic, but the present impasse of empires does not seem to be realistic, and we might seek with all deliberate speed to find more humane and politically viable alternatives.

It seems to me that, in their recent pastoral letters, the American Catholic bishops have been exemplary in their use of religious language to speak to public concerns. Both of the letters I cite draw centrally from the imagery of the kingdom of God. In the 1983 Pastoral Letter on War and Peace, the bishops begin with a section entitled ''Peace and the Kingdom,'' in which they say,

> As disciples and as children of God, it is our task to seek for ways in which to make the forgiveness, justice and mercy and love of God visible in a world where violence and enmity are too often the norm. When we listen to God's word, we hear again and always the call to repentance and to belief: to repentance because though we are redeemed we continue to need redemption; to belief, because although the reign of God is near, it is still seeking its fullness.[36]

---

[35]See Walter Russell Mead, *Mortal Splendor: The American Empire in Transition* (Boston: Houghton Mifflin, 1987), for a helpful analysis.

[36]*The Challenge of Peace: God's Promise and Our Response,* A Pastoral Letter on War and Peace, National Conference of Catholic Bishops, 3 May 1983, 17-18.

The 1986 Pastoral Letter on Catholic Social Teaching and the U.S. Economy closes with a section entitled "Commitment to a Kingdom of Love and Justice," in which the bishops say,

> The fulfillment of human needs, we know, is not the final purpose of the creation of the human person. We have been created to share in the divine life through a destiny that goes far beyond our human capabilities and before which we must in all humility stand in awe. . . . We have to move from our devotion to independence, through an understanding of interdependence, to a commitment to human solidarity. That challenge must find its realization in the kind of community we build among us. Love implies concern for all—especially the poor—and a continued search for those social and economic structures that permit everyone to share in a community that is a part of a redeemed creation. (Rom. 8:21- 23).[37]

Of course, those injunctions do not tell us exactly what to do, although both letters have many valuable suggestions about possible implementation. But their highest value—and in this they are exemplary of the place of the language of faith in public life—is to remind us that there is a larger stage on which we perform our public action and that the final judgment does not belong to us.

---

[37]*Economic Justice for All,* A Pastoral Letter on Catholic Social Teaching and the U.S. Economy, National Conference of Catholic Bishops, 18 November 1986, 182- 83.

The Kingdom of God in America

Alida Brill, responder

I write as a member of that minority gender present neither at the signing nor during the deliberations leading to the signing. But more significantly I speak from the perspective of a member of the minority religion—perhaps the mother religion, but not the dominant religion then or now of most Americans. I think it is probably the tradition of unheard voices that, when we finally get our chance, we tend to raise questions and cause a little trouble. I will try not to do too much of that, but I think that my brief comments here will be more in the way of questions and issues than in a direct response to Professor Bellah's excellent chapter.

I pose some questions about what I see is the fundamental quandary we find ourselves in when we dare to speak of religion and public life. We must move from the historic celebration of the Constitution, the reality and sacred myths of that time that we cherish, and come instead to the present day and ask what religion and the public good can possibly mean to us. The century in which the Constitution was drafted and signed was the century that had, at its base, what we now want to believe, I think, was an elegance of religion. Because of my past work on the Constitution, I have been following all the birthday parties that have been held in Philadelphia. And it seems to me that the Constitution is a tapestry long in its weaving. And when we try to reach the inner meaning or the original intent, we must by necessity seek to unweave it or unravel it. And I think if we could ultimately unravel it in our attempt to understand it, we would lose much of the picture of the tapestry. And yet I think that is what all of us who try to comment on the Constitution during its two-hundredth birthday are about. And I often think we are unweaving a picture still emerging, which makes it even more difficult.

Bellah's chapter raises one of the most thorny and troublesome themes in American society: the degree to which religion can or should be a public or a private matter, the notion of religion as a communal activity as opposed to religion as an act of solitude. Certainly the colonials banded together in religious community. But perhaps they did so as much for defense against others who did not believe exactly what they did, as the historian Leonard Levy has pointed out, as they did for a feeling of unity with one another. Yet, from Luther forward, and even before, we as humans have been confronted with a conflicting value of religion as a private, intimate, faithful act with a divine being or as an ideological, theological framework that mandates a certain kind of behavior in our public life. When Bellah mentions the notion of a God of good, of religions in his conception of nation, of empire, of community, I think we must also ask whether this is a grammar far removed from that "good citizen" of classic times.

The good citizen of classic times had defined a fairly rigid set of protocols, which, if followed, publicly proclaimed him or her a good citizen working for the common good. When colonials such as John Winthrop urged his followers to "knit together in this work as one man" and then ended with the famous "city upon a hill" quotation, I would argue that this model, while not diminishing its New Testament origins, is also Athenian. From my perspective, it is more Athenian than it is Judaic. What is troubling for America in these closing years of the twentieth century is that the translation of this kind of rhetoric into the mouths of political candidates and elected leaders can lead, not to the re-creation of Athens or the colonial spirit, or the community that Jesus was referring to, but to a kind of domestic and foreign policy that is not rooted at all in treating each person like a brother or sister.

While Bellah duly notes that the use of religious language in public discourse, though legitimate, has pitfalls, he does stop short, I believe, of some of its more vexing sorrows. I am myself guilty of the unforgivable sin of having spent too much of my time, as a survey researcher, asking people what they *believed* about America themselves. But I can sadly report that those who identify themselves as the most religious are often the least civically identified or the least civically interested.

At its worst, some of these citizens are those among us most likely to wish to snuff out the liberties of others. Why might this be so? I think it is because, increasingly, we live in a society that makes vast demands on our intellectual abilities and on our sense of ethics. In fact, I think our ethical scales are tipped with the overload of having to decide what is right, what is moral, and what is humane.

Issues that were never contemplated before in private are now broadcast over the news at the dinner hour. Humans look for a way to decode these events. In Robert Merton's terms, we look for a social theory or a structure of norms, a structure to guide our behavior, to tell us what is appropriate to believe, what is wrong, what is sinful. For many, religion, in its most narrow and restricted format, provides these norms. It influences and directs our values and our behavior. For those who ascribe to a set of beliefs from a creed that says there is only one way of believing, one way of finding truth in God, one way of achieving the kingdom of God, a set of behavior, values, and attitudes emerges that could hardly be described as loving, compassionate, or tolerant.

Because of the tenacity to which some hold onto these values of the higher order, we still find pockets of racial hatred and of anti-Semitism, this fear of difference among those who define themselves as believers. In making such remarks, I know that this is not the tradition of Christ Church, nor present in the history held in its walls or in the spirits of the Signers, who might still be interested enough in this great American experiment to somehow be with us now. But it cannot be overlooked that the recent course of history indicates that a direct causal line cannot be drawn from religion to patriotism to a pluralistic society. There are, however, models of democratic reciprocity, liberty, and egalitarianism and, indeed, the outlines of a road map for a civilized society in the pages of the Bible. And I think that guidance cannot be forgotten or denied.

Bellah's treatment of the importance of the Exodus in its imagery for the colonials is an important illustration of my previous point. However, I think perhaps the most critical aspect of his chapter, and one that resonates most directly for me, is the difference between *covenant* and *contract.*

Historian Arthur Herzberg has also made such a distinction. The covenant at Sinai (and let us not forget the covenant with Abraham) was the most specific kind of covenant from a God to his people. I argue that this notion of covenant rushes into a headlong and nasty collision with a notion of contract or, in our case, of constitution between a nation and its forefathers. It is this mixing of covenant and contract, or covenant and constitution, that I see as problematic in our modern day and that I believe leaves us still searching for the meaning of religion in the life of the good citizen.

The religious acts of the Christian Women United for Peace and the religious commitment behind the bishop's letters suggest that we may find that connection. The religious zealots who are also bigots and those intolerant of cultural or racial differences say that we have not found that connection. Bellah has indicated to us in his chapter the difference between the religious state and the just state that is guided by religious principle. I quote from an article by Herzberg, which appeared in the Catholic journal *Commonweal,* entitled, ''The Case for Untidyness.''

> Any state which enters the realm of our souls had better be one that God himself makes at the end of our days. If we would attempt to make a godly kingdom, it almost always becomes the engine of someone's oppression. What we have learned, painfully, in recent centuries is that we live best in untidyness with a decent concern for the opinions of all people—even as this costs many of us as believers something very precious to our own souls. In the West, even in an unbelieving 20th century, what we tend to define, by consent does bear relationship to the Biblical roots of our common culture and yet we cannot and must not stretch this too far to force the conscience of one or another branch of society.

Bellah, in his midrash on Niebuhr, concludes precisely where we need to conclude in this century: we must look to the depth of faith, not to the superficiality of language or religious rhetoric, for the achievement of the classic good society. Or in Niebuhr's terms, ''the kingdom of God," which I would amend to "the kingdom of God writ large," to expand all with this interface. If one moves from a kind of mindless mouthing of creed, as we unfortunately can witness so often in the most fundamental and uncompromising sects of both Judaism and Christianity, to the use of faith as analog, as Bellah has stated, it may be that the covenant/contract dichotomy, which is so problematic, can be less sharply divided. And then that private soul can be brought into the light for the public good. I think this direction aptly illustrates its possibility in two pastoral letters that were quoted. Finally, I conclude with what Abraham Joshua Heschel wrote in his volume *God in Search of Man*.

> It is customary to blame secular science and anti-religious philosophy for the eclipse of religion in modern society. It would be much more honest to blame religion for its own defeats. Religion declined, not because it was refuted, but because it became irrelevant, dull, oppressive, insipid. When faith is completely replaced by creed, worship by discipline, love by habit, when the crisis today is ignored by the splendor of the past, when faith is simply an heirloom, rather than a living fountain, when religion speaks only in the name of authority rather than in the strong voice of compassion, its message becomes meaningless. Religion should be the answer to man's ultimate questions.

The Kingdom of God in America

Robert F. Drinan, S.J., responder

I have always been skeptical and indeed somewhat hostile to the concept of a civil religion. I have followed the literature about this topic for at least twenty years and find myself almost resenting those who embrace civil religion or even those who try to analyze it. During the ten years I served in Congress, I sought almost scrupulously to avoid any of the rhetoric about the need for some kind of religion to be favored and even promoted by the state as the necessary foundation for public morality.

My resistance to any form of civil religion derives in part from my upbringing as a Catholic in a society that was pan-Protestant. I participated in a public high school in the recitation of the Twenty-third Psalm and the other public pieties that were common at that time.

But I never thought that the state's favoring or promoting religion was very important. I was troubled by the ban on prayers and Bible reading by the Supreme Court in 1963. But I have generally accepted the position taken by the Supreme Court on excluding religious symbols and services from public schools. Indeed, I find it hard to justify the Supreme Court's acquiescence to chaplains in state legislatures who are compensated by public funds.

Consequently, I have not lamented the disappearance of vaguely Protestant or Christian symbols and practices in America's public life.

I have generally recoiled at prayers offered at political or patriotic events. I resisted and resented the use or the exploitation of religion for objectives that may or may not be useful. At the same time, however, I have been deeply concerned that there be a source of public morality in America that could be adequate to do the things I want America to do, such as offering aid to the 600 million people who are chronically malnourished across the world.

As a result I resonate to Dr. Bellah's warning that "it is a doubtful and dangerous enterprise to use the language of faith as a language of nation and certainly as a language of empire." But I am pleased—indeed exhilarated—to see the praise that Bellah has for the language and the message of America's Catholic bishops in their 1983 pastoral letter on war and peace. I was pleased also to see his praise for the approach of the Catholic bishops in their 1986 pastoral on social teaching.

As I look back over the public piety that has flowed and flowered in American life until very recently, I am somewhat ashamed, a bit embarrassed, and seldom very pleased or proud. I cringe when I come across the flaming statements of the prohibitionists as they divided counties and states into wet and dry. I am generally appalled at the rise since 1980 of the rhetoric and pomposity of the Moral Majority and the religious fundamentalists. Consequently, I am reluctant to give much praise at all to those religious voices in the past that place the approval of religion behind a particular social or political movement.

I want, therefore, in this year of the bicentennial, to reexamine what the First Amendment tried to do and to assess how the Supreme Court has interpreted that amendment in the last forty years. My approach is that of a lawyer who is acutely sensitive to the demands and aspirations of non-Christians and post-Christians in America. I will review the legal and moral implications of the sixteen words of the First Amendment as they have been applied to American life over the last two hundred years.

The Constitution drawn up by fifty-three Protestant and two Catholic men in Philadelphia in 1787 made no reference to God or to religion except the provision in Article 6 that no religious test shall be required for any public office. The new federal government was to play no role, either for or against religion.

The authors of the double-edged First Amendment wanted to ensure that neither the government nor the churches dominated society. The ban on the establishment of religion thus fulfilled the desire of Roger Williams, who in 1636 fled from Massachusetts to seek religious freedom in Rhode Island, that there be a separation of church and state, lest the state dominate the churches. The establishment clause similarly responded to the fear of Thomas Jefferson that the churches might dominate the state.

If there is any one concept on which the Constitution and the First Amendment are clear, it is the notion that the state and the churches should be neither partners nor enemies. Somewhere in between there is an appropriate relationship. Scholars have used oceans of ink to discover the correct name. Is it benign neutrality? Accommodation? A cooperative separation?

In 1963, I published a book entitled *Religion, The Courts, and Public Policy* (McGraw-Hill), urging that the First Amendment permits and even requires some governmental subsidies for the secular parts of church-related schools. That approach is the position still advocated by the U.S. Catholic Conference on behalf of the nation's three hundred Catholic bishops. As a member of Congress I had no real occasion to vote on the issue. But I am not certain that the series of arguments that I used back in the 1960s are persuasive today. The Supreme Court has solidified its position on no aid.

Although there is no record that the Framers prayed together (they once adroitly declined Benjamin Franklin's invitation to do so), the first generation of leaders in the new nation introduced Protestant or at least deistic piety into American public life. Proclamations of Thanksgiving, the legalization of Christmas as a holiday, prayers before every session of Congress, and Bible reading and prayers in the public schools were but a few of the practices introduced in a nation whose Constitution had theoretically separated the realms of God and Caesar. The churches enjoyed tax exemption, the clergy were given preferential status, and the words *under God* were inserted into the Pledge of Allegiance.

An unchallenged and even unquestioned symbiosis between government and religion existed in America between 1787 and 1945. It was an extraordinary consensus epitomized by the McGuffey reader, filled with vaguely Protestant piety, which was widely used in the public schools. Nostalgia for that era, often embroidered and romanticized, is at the root of those who today want to "get God back into the public school."

Catholics were the largest group that did not feel themselves to be a part of the widely accepted feeling that the public school reflected and adequately transmitted the ideas of the Constitution and the ideals of America's religious heritage. In 1852, the Catholic bishops decreed that every parish should establish a school, to which all parents were required to send their children. Catholics were frowned upon, and their schools were denied virtually all tax support. Indeed, it took a decision of the United States Supreme Court in 1925 (*Pierce* v. *Society of Sisters*) to set aside a referendum of the people of Oregon that would have forbidden the very existence of private or Catholic schools.

In the 1940s, the enrollment in Catholic schools reached four million, or about 50 percent of all Catholic children. In 1947, the U.S. Supreme Court, really for the first time, had to decide whether the ban on the establishment of religion in the First Amendment precluded even the incidental aid of bus transportation for children attending Catholic schools. In a 5-4 split in the *Everson* decision, the Court allowed the bus rides but drew the line against any additional aid. In 1968, the Supreme Court allowed the loan of secular textbooks to pupils in Catholic schools. But in a long line of decisions from *Everson* in 1947 to a ban on shared time or dual enrollment in 1985, the Supreme Court has consistently and coherently ruled that the government may not give financial assistance to schools that are operated by a religious group. The 1985 decision, also 5-4, declared unconstitutional a plan carried out with federal funds since 1965 by which students in Catholic, Orthodox Jewish, and similar schools receive remedial or compensatory training on the school premises. Attempts to continue such training off the school premises are now being developed.

From 1947 to 1980, I participated in dozens of public debates or forums on the question of governmental aid to church-related schools. I sensed that many non-Catholics were moving to a position of being willing to grant what Catholic parents were requesting. They recognized that anti-Catholicism was clearly a factor in the denial of aid to Catholic schools and that, furthermore, Catholic and other sectarian schools receive substantial aid in other pluralistic pan-Protestant countries such as England, Canada, and Australia.

But I saw that empathy evaporate by the sharp rise in the late 1970s of hundreds of evangelical or fundamentalist schools in the South and Southwest. A new and unprecedented political twist was added when the Republican party in 1980 agreed to alter its platform by adding a pledge to seek to enact tuition tax credits for parents with children in private schools. The thought of financing the thousands of schools established by fundamentalist Protestant preachers like the Reverend Jerry Falwell chilled the feeling of my many debate opponents who were beginning to think that perhaps the Catholics had a point when they complained about the burden of supporting their own parochial schools while being taxed to finance public schools.

Meanwhile, the Supreme Court, beginning in 1948 with the *McCollum* decision, forbade religious teaching, Bible reading, or the recitation of a prayer in the public schools. Again the line of decisions is consistent and coherent. In 1985, even a moment of silence, if intended to permit prayer, was forbidden.

Hence the central question in the year of the bicentennial of the Constitution is this: Does the Constitution and the First Amendment require what the Supreme Court has mandated since it decided *Everson* in 1947 and *McCollum* in 1948? Or, as some commentators would put it: Does the Constitution require that all tax-supported schools be operated by the government and that, in these schools, there be no religious exercises at all?

The authors of the Constitution and the First Amendment never pondered this problem, because virtually every school in 1787 was operated by the churches; the public school with compulsory attendance was hardly even thought of prior to the establishment in 1837 of the first state board of education in Massachusetts, with Horace Mann as its secretary. So one's answer to the question, however it is phrased, depends on one's idea of the role religion should play in a pluralistic society. Answers to that riddle range from the strict separationist, to whom no aid means no aid, to the born-again Christian, who proclaims that, since God is the author of our Constitution, the nation should restore God to the center of our life.

Somewhere in between these viewpoints is the compelling but mushy concept that the state should "encourage" religion because, after all, our public morality flows from it. Official governmental encouragement for religion reached an unprecedented level in the Reagan administration. The decibels of presidential rhetoric have risen, but to more and more post-Christians and non-Christians the claims that America is a nation grounded in the Judeo-Christian tradition seem hollow, hypocritical, and even a bit dangerous. The more ardent apostles of this view sometimes declaim that the lamentable increase in divorce, delinquency, abortion, and pornography could be curbed if the government put its institutional strength behind religion. The concealed premise underlying this view is the conviction that both religion and government will be stronger if government openly, or at least subtly, helps to advance the objectives of religion. But the idea that government should be a partner of religion contains the dangerous idea that religion will be weakened if it is not supported by the state. That idea, of course, is a pervasive one going back to Constantine in Christian times. Church leaders regularly forget that, if they accept the patronage of secular rulers, these politicians will in due course almost inevitably demand of the churches an allegiance that the churches can offer only to God.

The argument is made again and again that the Founding Fathers never intended to privatize religion by keeping it out of the nation's principal institution for the transmission of moral values—its schools. The Congress sought to meet these pressures when in 1985 it passed the Equal Access Act. Under this law student-initiated religious exercises in high school may be conducted on school property during hours assigned for other cocurricular student activities. No hard information is yet available as to what impact, if any, this new law is having.

The Constitution was designed in certain ways to privatize religion in the sense that it sought to do away with the abuses of the publicly established religious regime in England. The Constitution and the First

Amendment were also intended to secularize society, at least in the sense that any vestiges of English and European theocracy were rejected. The undeniable fact is that the United States Constitution with its First Amendment was a bold and unique experiment in regulating the almost always turbulent clashes between government and religions. In the United States those clashes were muted and even precluded by the creation of a society that does not establish religion but grants the free exercise of religion to all its adherents.

It is a delicate balance—to deny aid to the churches but to grant religious freedom to their members. Under this formula church-related schools have not received financing, nor have religious practices been permitted in the public schools. But religious freedom has been almost universally available. What more should believers want from their government?

////The Kingdom of God in America////////////////////////////
/////////////////////////////////// Christopher F. Mooney, S.J., responder////

Robert Bellah has long been a voice in America calling for the reentry into our public conversation of biblical values and themes as well as of traditional American concerns for civic responsibility and public service. This he has done because he is seeking some antidote to the limitations we have unwittingly imposed upon this public conversation by our current moral vocabulary of personal self-fulfillment and financial success. His recent collaborative book *Habits of the Heart* sees our biblical and republican traditions receding into the background, their languages eroded by an expressive and instrumental individualism that has become our dominant language today.

"Cultures," he believes, "are dramatic conversations about things that matter to their participants, and American culture is no exception." What used to matter to Americans was our efforts as a nation to realize the ancient biblical hope of a just and compassionate society, as well as to shape our lives in accord with the ideals of republican citizenship. Today what matters much more to us is our third tradition, our spirit of enterprise and our right to amass for ourselves wealth and power. Unless this insistent emphasis upon self-interest is modified, Bellah says, we shall as citizens develop more and more fragmented lives and become less and less able to recognize that human happiness and self-fulfillment must also include involvement in civic life and relationships to others in community. The key to this recognition is the public retrieval of our two neglected languages, because, as he says, "American culture remains alive so long as conversation continues and the argument is intense."

But appropriating religious language into our public discourse entails certain risks, which I take to be the main burden of Bellah's chapter. The question he poses, after his very enlightening historical overview, is whether our biblical tradition can indeed be spoken in public today without involving us once again in blindness and complacency before the massive moral ambiguities of nation and empire. His tentative answer is that it can. He cites the example of Martin Luther King, Jr., whose religious inspiration provided a moral vision that permanently changed our institutions and transformed our culture. And he cites the recent pastoral letters of the American Catholic bishops, dealing with moral dilemmas in the economy and in nuclear deterrence, as examples of how to reflect responsibly in religious language on public concerns.

My problem with this tentative answer of his is that it is not tentative enough. On the negative side, Bellah cites only President Reagan's propensity to use religious language to castigate evil empires and congratulate us on our own righteousness, but his historical analysis makes it clear that he would surely recognize a much greater risk today than vacuous appeals from public officials. I think this present risk needs to be spelled out. I see it coming from three different sources, all of them religious.

The first is a militant form of fundamentalism, symbolized by the Moral Majority but reaching very broadly into American sectarianism. This antimodern religious subculture looks back with nostalgia to a more ordered and homogeneous world where religion meant consensus on private morality and naive patriotic conviction that our country could do no wrong. Its members now hunger for a nationwide authority, certainty, inerrancy, and strict moral conformity—in short, for an unpluralistic America. Their communitarianism is strong but also highly privatized. In recent years they have not hesitated to assert their convictions in the public sphere, belligerently, intolerantly, and without civility, convinced that their religious values and theirs alone must be normative for the nation. What they mean by religion in public life has also been sharply focused: the criminalization of abortion, legalization of prayer in public schools, opposition to feminism and the rights of homosexuals, and the prohibition of busing to achieve racial integration. Their use of religious language in public thus has as its aim not to converse about policies but to impose them.

There is another sectarian movement in America today that, unlike fundamentalism, is theologically sophisticated and critical, free of rigidities and open to ecumenical dialogue. Nevertheless, it constitutes a second source of risk because its aim is to avoid the public sphere altogether and to have nothing to do with national debate. Its adherents, often referred to as "postliberal," do not believe that religion can ever really change society and ought not to be in the business of trying. They argue that, since all understandings of right and wrong have to be community based, Christian churches should not presume that they can ever be understood by the secular world, or perhaps even by each other. The Christian story, in other words, is irreducibly particular, and can be heard only by those who can speak its biblical language. The postliberals are therefore extremely pessimistic about any effort to reach shared meanings in the secular sphere. This new form of Protestant sectarianism has recently appeared in Roman Catholic form in the Vatican censure of Hans Küng and Charles Curran. Here, however, the issue is the incommunicability of ecclesiastical, not biblical, language. For the Catholic sectarian, theology is a domestic not a public undertaking, whose natural home is the church not the academy. Since the purpose of such ecclesiastical language for the sectarian is to explain and defend official hierarchical positions, its use to critique these positions by dialoguing in the public sphere must be rejected as a threat to sectarian identity.

The third source of risk comes from the mainline churches, from a problem endemic to all of them—namely, the unavoidable difficulty of translating the religious language of any one tradition into terms accessible to those outside that tradition. I am speaking now, it should be noted, of churches that stand ready and eager to search together with other churches for common religious understandings of public events. Obviously the point of departure in such searching must be some given denominational base, since we are dealing here with people trying to be faithful to the visions and values of their own community. Public argument, however, either with other religious groups or with judicial and legislative bodies, can never be fruitful unless proposals for shared meanings are intelligible apart from the particular religious experience that was their origin. Mainline churches are still not adept at this task of translation. We need only to recall Bellah's remarks on the multiple meanings of "kingdom of God" for Americans to recognize the extent of the problem.

We have today, then, three very different religious approaches to public conversation. Unfortunately, the genuine communitarianism of the two sectarian approaches can never be socially transformative, because neither is interested in new possibilities for public moral insight or political choice. In the case of the fundamentalists, religious values are already prepackaged, to be taken or left; in the case of the postliberals, these values are presumed to be incommunicable and so never brought into discussion at all. Such intolerance and withdrawal are equally fatal to public discourse. But mainline churches have their own language problem. Obstacles to good translation still too often inhibit them from breaking out of their micromoralities into public moral positions wide-reaching enough to grapple with the larger questions of the commonwealth. The two pastoral letters of the Catholic bishops are indeed examples of such a wide-reaching macromorality, but I see them as the exceptions, not the rule.

I strongly agree with Bellah that we will continue to have a society that is off-balance and skewed toward affluence and narcissism unless we introduce as correctives into our public discourse languages that speak of transcendent values and public service. The point of my response to him is that the religious situation in America today ought to make us aware that, when we attempt to introduce biblical concepts into the public realm, the risk we are taking is very great indeed. Churches as a group may simply not be up to it; or they may bungle the job badly, as they have often done in the past; or, worst of all, they may once again allow the task to be perverted by public officials only too eager to speak the deeds of nation and empire in words of high morality and faith.

From a human point of view, therefore, looking at the situation sociologically, I think I would be more pessimistic than Bellah is about this enterprise. Looking at the situation theologically, however, I think I am perhaps more willing than he to trust this whole matter to the providence of God. Toward the end of his chapter he has a single, almost parenthetical sentence: "Of course, empires too exist under the sovereignty of God and may sometimes . . . work for good." I conclude these remarks with a much stronger affirmation than that.

If God is to be God, then I believe that God's creative and salvific action must be seen as present to all human experience, whether secular or sacred. No human institution, in other words, however sinful, is an autonomous structure in which God has no interest, since every human institution influences the way people live in society, which in turn influences the way they think about God and their neighbor. To speak of the kingdom of God in America must mean, at the very minimum, that God is somehow *there*. The fact that secular institutions are never found to be all good, that most are indeed ambiguous, a mix of good and bad (some very bad), is simply a reflection of the human condition. The prior concern of the religious person is thus not what she or he should be doing in secular life but what God might be doing. For before any individual pursues human development, God pursues it. Before any individual promotes freedom and equality, God does.

This line of thinking does not imply that human institutions can ever escape frustration and even subversion from human sinfulness. It is simply to assert that they are human and, as such, objects of a divine will. Though ultimately the purpose of God's providential design is salvific, the union of all persons with God's own self in the sphere of the sacred, God's immediate creative purposes in the secular sphere must be secular, that is, in conformity with the nature of any given institution. These purposes may be shrouded in mystery, but they are carried out nonetheless through the meshing of divine providence with human prudence, through the instrumentality of men and women whose prudential judgments in the secular world further any given providential design. History is thus not simply a course of human events but a series of dramatic encounters between the human and the divine.

Just over a decade ago a clergyman in Philadelphia heard that two authors were writing a book entitled *Defining America*. He wrote them with a question: "Can you give me some help in my effort to be *proud* of my country again?" Bellah has spoken to this felt need in all of us with admirable realism. That realism tells us that we Americans are probably never going to be able to think and talk of our nation religiously without keeping one eye on our individual and national self-interest. Nevertheless, we can still cherish a religious ideal for our public conversation, even as we acknowledge the relativity of its fulfillment. We all know the harm that has been done by public use of biblical tradition: it has fostered the myth of messianic America and the moral absolutes of empire. But we also know that only this tradition can give us language strong enough to speak to our blindness as a nation and to our perennial failure to achieve a just society. So we have no choice but to use this language. I would only hope that, whenever we do, we also recognize that we are not alone, but acting always under the ever-watchful judgment and sovereignty of God.

Church, State, and Religious Freedom

Citizens of the United States use code language borrowed from Europe when they speak of "church" and "state." America does not have "church." It has "churches," or "religions," or "religious people." The Supreme Court has decided that the United States Constitution protects not only the freedom of the "church." In *Welsh* v. *United States,* 398 U.S. 333 (1970), it has gone as far as to protect a person's "moral, ethical, or religious beliefs about what is right and wrong," provided those beliefs be held with the strength of traditional religious convictions."

Similarly, America does not have "state" in the inherited European sense. Even constitutionally, it has "states" and a federal union that makes up a nation. In any case, there is no single authority called "state" to represent the civil power the way, in the Middle Ages, emperor faced off against or linked up with pope, prince stood across from or next to bishop, and so on. Indeed, the Constitution and the Bill of Rights use neither term. Thomas Jefferson, in his famed letter to the Danbury, Connecticut, Baptist Association, gave permanence to the terms when he spoke of "a wall of separation between church and state."

Students of the Constitution and the writings and concepts of the Founders and Framers have preferred James Madison's phrase pointing to the two areas: "the line of separation between the rights of religion and the civil authority.'' Historian Sidney E. Mead resurrected that phrase and gave it new life.[1] Its great virtue is that it deals more realistically with the American situation, for a line allows for more fluidity, viscosity, and adaptation than does the more concrete metaphor of a wall.

In popular speech, however, Jefferson still wins out, and the canon and code call for us to discuss issues of ''church'' and ''state.'' The best we can do is to keep mental quotation marks around the two terms, thus allowing for historically nuanced, legally textured, and practically open approaches to a complex set of realities. The issues of church and state pose some of the most tense, puzzling, and conflictual problems for the whole society.

// A Problem of Insubordination

Most discussions of church and state begin with models of parity. Yet, in a constitutional republic, hard as it may be for religionists to swallow, church and religion have to be subordinate or subordinated to state and civil authority. One can go many years in fields where church and state receive mention and never hear about this primal notion. One scholar who has brought it to view in recent times, Walter Berns, all but rubbed in the notion of subordinateness in order to make certain neoconservative points about the Constitution and property, or about the reliance of the Framers not on ''God'' but on ''the state of nature.''

Thus, writes Berns, ''The Constitution was ordained and established to secure liberty and its blessings, not to promote faith in God. Officially, religion was subordinate to liberty and was to be fostered . . . only with a view to securing liberty.'' Furthermore, ''the origin of free government in the modern sense coincides with and can *only* coincide with, the solution of the religious problem, and the solution of the religious problem consists in the subordination of religion.'' Once more, ''Americans had . . . succeeded in combining the spirit of religion and

---

[1]Sidney E. Mead, *The Nation with the Soul of a Church* (New York: Harper and Row, 1975) 79.

the spirit of liberty, but they did so by subordinating the former to the latter."[2]

That religion is civilly and, shall we say, constitutionally subordinate is obvious to any citizen who makes a few tests. Think about who grants whom charters. The churches go to the state for decrees and charters that make them civilly legitimated institutions, especially for purposes of tax exemption. Churches work toward and appeal for a law for conscientious objection to military service. They have to abide by police regulations and fire ordinances and work within the stipulations of a civil zoning board. They ask to get out of taxes, as the state never need ask to get out of a stewardship drive. Their members can be guilty of treason, while the civil authority cannot effectively suffer even so much as stigma for having been guilty of heresy.

Subordination, however, means subordination in the legal sense and nothing more. To be subordinate is to be "subject to the authority or control of another." When I called attention to this meaning in a recent lecture, a respondent heard wrong: "You of all people," he replied, "should be the last to say that the church should be subservient to the state." And so I would be. While the two terms are connected, subservient means "useful as a means or instrument," which is all right so far as it goes, but it carries the connotation in dictionaries of "obsequious; servile."

Religious persons and their institutions have a right to be "useful as a means of instrument." William Lee Miller has shown how ready the eighteenth-century civil authorities were to see religion as a public utility, so that there might be a "religion works" to match the "water works" and the "gas works."[3] They may even be obsequious and servile, as the record often shows them being. But most religions define themselves as other than subservient. They see themselves responsive to a "higher law." Religious protest acquires a certain dignity that even

---

[2]Walter Berns, *The First Amendment and the Future of American Democracy* (New York: Basic, 1976) 15, 26, 32.

[3]William Lee Miller, *The First Liberty: Religion and the American Republic* (New York: Knopf, 1986) 28.

its enemies have to deal with and sometimes covertly admire when believers, out of deep conviction, suffer for that conviction where it does not match the boundaries of civil law. From Mohandas Gandhi through Martin Luther King to Soviet dissidents, such people have come to be admired in our time. Such expression of conviction amounts to at least momentary insubordination, often for the purpose of restoring to law a dignity that it might have been losing when it was protecting injustice.

Protecting the nonsubservient believers and institutions is one of the great purposes of the religion clause of the First Amendment, as applied now by the United States Supreme Court to the practices of individual states. The amendment exercises this protection through two means. On one hand, "Congress shall make no law respecting the establishment of religion." In the ever-broadening sense with which this clause has been interpreted, it means that the civil authority is not to establish or give privilege to a church, churches, religion, or religions in such a way that other religions or nonreligion is discriminated against and forced to be not subordinate but subservient. In phrases of the Court, the government is to be "benevolently" or "wholesomely" neutral in respect to religion.

The other clause is more directly to the point: "Congress shall make no law . . . prohibiting the free exercise [of religion]." We shall take up this free exercise guarantee first, for historically it was seen to be most directly connected with our topic, religious freedom. To this day the free exercise clauses involving individuals or small bodies usually pose the most dramatic if not the civilly most rich cases.

// Free Exercise Thereof

The drafters, signers, and ratifiers of the Constitution and the First Amendment had good reason to protect the free exercise of religion. For centuries in the West, men and women who would not be spiritually subservient had suffered from an encroaching civil authority, one that demanded religious uniformity within careful boundaries. From the time of Constantine in the fourth century to James Madison in the eighteenth, almost everywhere Christians in that West, in Europe and its American derivative, were established and privileged to the exclusion of others.

Jews could exist in ghettos, Muslims across the Mediterranean, sectarians in remote mountain fastnesses, and infidels not at all.

In colonial America the same situation was to have prevailed to some degree or other in nine of the thirteen colonies, where establishment and privilege had led to limits on free exercise of religion. Quakers had been hounded and hanged. Baptists complained that they had to pay taxes for another religion in which they did not believe or for religions and religiousness when they did not think government should be any sort of instrument for propping up or promoting faith. In colony after colony, now state after state, these dissenters had been winning ever-broader freedoms for free exercise. Still, the constitutionalists had to pay attention to their needs.

In a perceptive essay first published in 1920, philosopher George Santayana argued that Americans got their liberties in two ways. First, there had to be "pensive or rabid apostles of liberty," for whom liberty "meant liberty for themselves to be just so, and to remain just so for ever." All the while they expressed "the most vehement defiance of anybody who might ask them, for the sake of harmony, to be a little different." Santayana knew their minds and souls. "Any one who passionately . . . believes in his particular religion cannot be content with less liberty . . . ; he must be free to live absolutely according to his ideal, and no hostile votes, no alien interests, must call on him to deviate from it by one iota. Such was the claim to religious liberty which has played so large a part in the revolutions and divisions of the western world."[4]

Balancing this pensiveness and rabidity, Santayana thought—and I think the historical record of constitutionalism bears this out—was a spirit that Santayana attributed to the English nature. (The national or ethnic tie we leave to other people on other days to examine, and will be content now to use it only again as a code name.) This "spirit of free cooperation" was rooted in "free individuality." It could help produce a cooperative Constitution: "We the people of the United States. . . " It issued in "the form of trust and adaptability," moving "by a series of

---

[4]George Santayana, *Character and Opinion in the United States* (Garden City NY: Doubleday, 1956) 119.

checks, mutual concessions, and limited satisfactions.'' Thus ''the passions, even in a rational society, remain the elements of life, but under mutual control, and the life of reason . . . is a perpetual compromise.'' Santayana concluded: ''English liberty, because it is co-operative, because it calls only for partial and shifting unanimity among living men, . . . is the best heritage of America.'' He went on, ''Certainly absolute freedom would be more beautiful if we were birds or poets; but co-operation and a loving sacrifice of a part of ourselves—or even of the whole, save the love in us—are beautiful too, if we are men living together.''[5]

Translate these observations to the reality of the Constitution framing, and it is clear that the Founders knew that a republic could not be made up, and was not made up, of nothing but several million absolutists going their passionate and uncompromising ways. Given the diversities within the population, the Constitution could not itself demand religious conformity or give formal expression to religion, as older charters, covenants, compacts, and constitutions had done with their characteristic openings: ''In the name of God. Amen.''

The best the Constitution could do about the latter issue was to be silent about God and religion. The Constitution is godless and even religionless; a meager but important reference says only that there will be no religious tests for public office. That is it. For the former issue, the First Amendment had to suffice: Congress should make no law prohibiting the free exercise of religion.

The free exercise cases almost always come up in abrasive social circumstances, where an individual or a small group offends the compromisers who have been helping assure public order. Jehovah's Witnesses parents scandalize the larger community by being ready to let their children die, apart from religiously prohibited blood transfusions. Members of the Unification church offend parents and siblings of members or larger circles in the society and are accused of ''brainwashing'' and ''mind control.'' Fundamentalist Baptists shock their neighbors by

---

[5]Ibid., 132, 141.

insisting that, for teachers in their parochial schools, there dare be not even licensing by state authorities.

While each case offends, somehow more often than not the courts and the public find ways to adapt and accommodate. Sometimes they do so almost prudentially. To give the state the authority to determine what a religious brainwash is in respect to Hare Krishna or the Unification church might be to turn that authority loose some day on Baptists who use considerable psychological inducement to produce "born-again" youth, or Catholics who engage in "formation" of nuns. Yet, beyond prudence, there is in the constitutional spirit, a sense of legal fair play and a sense that "free exercise" should be extended as far as possible. Many of us have signed amicus curiae briefs supporting on constitutional grounds the legal rights of religionists whose creed and practice we find thoroughly offensive.

Today "free exercise" is taken for granted by most citizens most of the time, even as they make room for fanatics or radicals, as they see them, who pensively or rabidly insist on their religious freedom to go their own way. Teachers of the constitutional tradition of religious freedom have considerable difficulty getting their students to see how radical the First Amendment liberties were. Does not everybody have free exercise? Is not the situation in the Soviet Union or in other totalitarian or authoritarian systems of left or right a momentary or novel invention? The fact that limits on free exercise of religion and thus on religious freedom were norms, standards, and almost universal practices up into and through most American colonial life is a reality that students find hard to picture.

Yet, the battle for "free exercise" was long and hard. The First Amendment to the Constitution could not settle everything; indeed, not everything has begun to be settled yet. Its framers could not anticipate all eventualities in our ever more pluralist society. The Framers had limited power: if they wanted the Bill of Rights ratified, they had to be content not to interfere with the states and to see to it only that "Congress" shall make no laws prohibiting free exercise of religion. Yet, it was a very great deed and moment in Western history when they constitutionally provided for religious liberties on a federal level never before guaranteed on such a scale elsewhere. They at least came up with a kind of working hypothesis of an expansively free society.

// No Establishment

The first clause of the First Amendment today is the subject of more debate, if not on a case-by-case basis, as in the case of free exercise instances, but in general. "Congress shall make no law respecting an establishment of religion." The debate has come up recently on some surprising, rather curious grounds. Not until the 1940s did the Supreme Court begin to apply stipulations of First Amendment religious freedom consistently to the states. The Court then employed the Fourteenth Amendment and the concept of "incorporation" as the instrument of doing so.

This movement by the Court is under attack in the 1980s by government officials as high as the attorney general. Some conservative historians, typically Robert L. Cord, have gone on intensely and at elaborate length in efforts to show that such "incorporation" violates what the attorney general calls "the intentions of the Founders" and is, in any case, bad law and bad for religion.[6] It would be tempting to get involved in the issue of incorporation, which is admittedly an extremely complex matter, but it would divert us into technical legal matters that would prevent us from exploring questions of ethos that preoccupy the United States at bicentennial time.

Let me move past the issue of the First and the Fourteenth amendments with but three asides. The first is bibliographical: a case countering Cord's but one that spends little time on the religion clause is a study by Michael Kent Curtis.[7] The second is of the "water over the dam" sort: after twoscore years of U.S. Supreme Court involvement with state-level First Amendment cases, these have become a part of the le-

---

[6]Robert L. Cord, *Separation of Church and State: Historical Fact and Current Fiction* (New York: Lambeth, 1982).

[7]Michael Kent Curtis, *No State Shall Abridge: The Fourteenth Amendment and the Bill of Rights* (Durham NC: Duke University Press, 1986).

gal tradition and have to be reckoned with, even as they will be built upon.

The third aside is to suggest that the "intentions of the Founders" argument works in several directions. Literary critics today like to remind us how difficult it is for anyone to know even one's own intentions, to say nothing of the intentions of others, especially the long dead, who cannot be interviewed. They go on to point to the limits of the historical relevance in any case: a text, once written, acquires a life of its own and becomes a part of its own interpretive history. Furthermore, few would want to go along with the "intentions of the Founders" in respect to many urgent issues, including the retention of slavery and the extension of the franchise to so few. Finally, the Framers were of many intentions, and their intentions in respect to religion, establishment, and free exercise cannot be simply condensed. In any case, we have the First Amendment and the Fourteenth Amendment and a U.S. Supreme Court ready to connect the two, as does the majority of the public.

Beyond that rather side-stepped legal-debate hurdle, there is still a long track and, with it, the question at which I hinted a moment ago: why is it controversial now? The reasons for the controversiality are generally positive, I would argue. They have to do less with the technical instance of the law and the land and more with the ethos that stands behind respect and support for it, on one hand. On the other, they have to do with widespread citizen regard for the spiritual and religious dimensions of a constitutional republic.

At midcentury it was more widely believed that Jefferson's "wall of separation between church and state" was all that one needed. Keep religion far from civil life and civil life far from religion, and all will be well. Religion is a private affair; its public dimensions should be generally hidden from view, sequestered, subjected to strictures and restrictions, and seen to be recessive, heading toward demise. America was simply a "secular society" that allowed for religious freedom for private citizens or, if they insisted on it, in their churches.

Today the climate has changed. For one thing, more observers are ready to say that we are not simply a secular society. While not all would agree with the second half of Justice William O. Douglas's dictum in

Zorach v. *Clauson,* 343 U.S. 306 (1952), that our "institutions pre-suppose a Supreme Being," most would agree with his first phrase, the historically based idea that "we are a religious people." We are some-how, in an inelegant term that I would prefer, a religiosecular people in a religiosecular society. Constitutional, civil, and religious thinking to-day tries to do justice to that reality.

Reasons for concern have grown as citizens have debated what lies behind a good civil society, a constitutional republic. The rea-soning goes something like this: Once the Founders decided to have a godless constitution, to be restrained in giving legal basis to a spe-cific revelation of God, Scripture, religious tradition, or established church, they had to find new grounds for support of law. It is one thing to say that one's sovereign speaks for The Sovereign God and that the majesty of law issues from it. It is another to begin, "We the people of the United States. . . . "

On such grounds, it is further argued, the Founders themselves in their abundant private writings believed that the Constitution would be observed and the republic remain healthy and free only if there was a virtuous people. The sequence was something on this order: the Con-stitution derives authority from an at least implicit and broad *consensus juris.* This is some sort of minimal agreement, on an expansive field, concerning the basis and background of law and observance. Such a *consensus juris* demanded civic or public virtue. That virtue was grounded in the private morality of the citizens. And, carrying it all one step further, most of the Founders argued that morality was somehow connected with religion.

How connected? Which religion? These questions have come to be a subject of intense debate in our time. Walter Berns speaks for those who argue that the *consensus juris* was grounded not in anything like Jewish or Christian revelation, Scripture, tradition, law, or observance. Had the Founders "intended to establish a Christian commonwealth," the only religious kind that, under the circumstances, would have been open to them, "it was remiss of them—indeed, sinful of them—not to have said so and to have acted accordingly. If they thought that all gov-ernment was derived from God, they would have been remiss in not establishing constitutional institutions calculated to help Americans to live according to His laws.'' Instead of this, ''the first of Madison's amendments, proposed in response to the demands of the states for a bill of rights, was a declaration insisting not that all power derives from God, but 'that all power is originally vested in, and consequently derives from, the people.' ''[8]

Berns goes on to say that, ''instead of establishing religion, the Founders established religious *freedom,* and the principle of religious freedom derives from a nonreligious source.'' Instead of a presupposed Supreme Being (pace Justice Douglas on a bad and uncharacteristic day), ''the institutions they established presuppose the rights of man, which were discovered . . . to exist prior to all government—in the state of nature, to be precise.'' And Berns rudely goes on to remind that ''the idea of the state of nature is incompatible with Christian doctrine.''[9]

Call this the secular-philosophical ''state of nature'' approach to the grounding of the *consensus juris.* Today it has few organized defenders; the heirs of eighteenth-century Enlightenment secular individualism are on the defensive, standing for something worth protecting constitutionally but not sure just what hit them in our ''postmodern'' and, some would say, postsecular situation.

A second school contributing to the *consensus juris*-civic virtue-morality-religion debate would say that ''the state of nature'' meant, for our very religious Founders, what John Adams called our ''one religion.'' And it centered in capitalized realities like Nature's God, Natural Law, Natural Rights, Natural Reason, something like Deism, the religion of what Henry F. May called ''the moderate Enlightenment'' and Sidney E. Mead called ''the religion of the republic.''

Rather than introduce a confusingly large cast of characters, let us revisit Mead for this second position, as we have revisited Berns for the first. Mead argues that, while private citizens are free to be members of denominations, what each sect holds separately is irrelevant to the pub-

---

[8]Berns, *First Amendment,* 11.

[9]Ibid., 15-16.

lic good. Only what they hold in common with the "religion of the Republic," the religion of Washington, Adams, Jefferson, Franklin, Madison, or almost any of the Founders, is relevant for public virtue and the *consensus juris*.

Mead, with tongue half in cheek and with ironic eye on what the churches held particularly, argued that they are irrelevant for their particularities and only when they hold something in common are they relevant directly to the public good. He argues that, behind the Constitution, there is a "theology [that] is not only *not* particularistic [as is all church theology, he claims]; it is designedly antiparticularistic." The Founders held that "only what is common to all religions and all sects—Franklin's 'essentials of every religion'—is relevant to the being and well-being of the *common*wealth." Then comes the twinkle, the taunt, or the irony: "This is the theology behind the legal structure of America, the theology on which the practice of religious freedom is based and its meaning interpreted. Under it, one might say, it is religious particularity, Protestant or otherwise, that is heretical and schismatic—even un-American!"[10]

Elsewhere Mead agrees with Crane Brinton that, in the seventeenth and eighteenth centuries, "there arose in our society what seems to be clearly a new religion. . . . I call this religion simply Enlightenment, with a capital E," a "religion of the republic" that "provides, or legitimates, the premises of the Declaration of Independence, the Constitution, and a long line of Supreme Court decisions on matters pertaining to religion." Mead argues that the Founders were neither particularist Christians who would ground the *consensus juris* in particular and, to many, inaccessible divine revelation nor secularist philosophers. In effect, they disestablished existing colonial Christian establishments in order to make room for their privileged Enlightenment faith. Here is a subordination not only of religious polities but of theologies: the civil authorities rely on what they determine are the es-

---

[10]Mead, *Nation with the Soul*, 22.

sentials of all religions, and they thus put the churches in their "heretical and schismatic—even un-American" places.[11]

One is not likely to get a much more forthright statement of "the religion of the republic" than this. It had been articulated on more secular grounds but with religious terminology decades earlier in John Dewey's concept of a nonsectarian, nonscriptural, not conventionally godded, but still somehow "common faith" (in which the symbol *God* could still appear). Walter Lippmann's "public philosophy" had relied on what Lippmann had called a "religion of the spirit," a nonchurchly sort, to back the *consensus juris* and develop morality and civic virtue. Somehow most Americans, when they come to debate the constitutional ethos, stop sounding either secular or individualist and are soon talking about some version of a common faith, a religious public philosophy, a religion of the republic.

When first articulated, around midcentury, the vestigial "one religion" that Adams had favored was a kind of blend of broad and liberal mainstream Protestantism with a relatively unarticulated version of this Enlightenment natural religion. Today that synthesis has broken. Protestant theologians in the neoorthodox seasons attacked the notion of natural law itself. Meanwhile, their churches were losing their hegemonous position in society. Catholics used different arguments for natural law and then, after the Second Vatican Council (1962–1965), began to waver in their argument about it or based on it. Asian, African, occult, cultic, "new" religions found their space under the constitutional sun and wanted their word in respect to *consensus juris* in the republic.

Most crucially, philosophical support for the "religion of the republic" weakened. It was hard to find an academic philosophy department that taught the "religion of the Enlightenment" as the truth about life. It belonged in history departments, where it was taught as a once nobly conceived but now seen to be metaphysically and linguistically condemned philosophical religion. It was cherished often by individualists to whom religion was a "private affair," but they did not know how to sustain a republic on such grounds.

---

[11]Ibid., 118.

On that terrain came newly articulate militant groups. Their common point of attack was the notion that the Founders *either* would have favored a Christian (now diplomatically translated as Judeo-Christian) commonwealth, had they foreseen our wild pluralism and moral chaos today, *or* that their heirs had bastardized what they stood for and now had built a counterestablishment. In this view, they had established, most of all in public elementary and high schools, an adversary to revealed religion, the "religion of secular humanism." By the late 1980s in some southern legislatures and courts, it was coming to be argued that all teaching that impinges on morality and civic virture that does *not* mention or call for faith in the God of Judeo-Christians was and had to be religious, a religion—the religion of secular humanism.

Why, they asked, should this religion be established or privileged? Why not at least allow for citizens to have "free exercise" in the face of it? This could mean that they be given tuition tax credits or vouchers so that they would have "freedom of choice" that would make possible private and parochial sectarian education. Or it could mean that, at this bicentennial date, "the Judeo-Christian tradition" should be privileged and taught as, somehow, the truth about life in public schools.

President Ronald Reagan, Attorney General Edwin Meese, and Secretary of Education William Bennett have gained support for this Judeo-Christian privilege view, as have some neoconservative publicists and great numbers of conservative Christian populists (often clumped simply under the banner New Christian Right, or fundamentalism). Not all are clear as to exactly how they would establish or privilege this tradition. By a constitutional amendment? By the rhetoric and practice of the republic, as when, in 1983, the president (as was his right) and the Congress (as, I would argue, was not its right) established "The Year of the Bible?" As a rider on education bills that forbid "the teaching of secular humanism" and the favoring of the Judeo-Christian? The consequences of the pro-Judeo-Christian rhetoric are not clear, except among the New Christian Right militants, who know exactly what they do not want and do want.

Whatever one thinks of the counterproposals, it is clear that, at bicentennial time, the debate over religious freedom has come back to the establishment clause. Historians in the proestablishment tradition have retraced their steps to the colonies and states and argued that the First Amendment, by keeping only Congress out of religious establishment, was making it possible for "nonpreferential" support of religion. (It is true that some Founders, George Washington and Patrick Henry among them, saw no incompatibility between their Enlightenment religion and the notion that the churches could themselves be state supported, as long as support was nonpreferential. Jefferson and Madison opposed that idea.) Leonard W. Levy has summoned all the arguments against nonpreferentialism, but the outcomes of the debate are by no means settled, if, indeed, they ever can be.[12]

Does America need a *consensus juris?* Can it resurrect the "state of nature" that Berns thought Founders relied on, or "Nature's God" and "the essentials of all religions" that Mead thought made up their creed? Or should the nation rely on the Judeo-Christian majority's tradition and ethos to develop this consensus? Almost any of these resolutions raises more problems than it solves. Let me spend just a moment on the notion of Judeo-Christian privilege by law and governmental favor.

It is often argued, by what strike me as the nostalgic minded, that we would have the necessary *consensus juris* if we would revert to the practices of "the good old days" when America had an agreed-upon moral fabric. One wonders. Find, for instance, the moment when more Americans in power agreed with each other on this assertion than at any other time. I would choose the high years of the Protestant empire, when more people gave assent to a common Bible in a common (King James) version; to belief in God the Father of Jesus Christ and unanimity on Christ's divine sonship; on heaven and hell and rewards and punishments and Moses-based, Jesus centered morality in an evangelical context. Then we would all agree? Then precisely we disagreed enough to have our bloodiest war, our Civil War, which was also a war over biblical interpretation.

---

[12]Leonard W. Levy, *The Establishment Clause: Religion and the First Amendment* (New York: Macmillan, 1986).

If the historical illustrations, of which that was only one, do not suffice, picture the contemporary situation. It is argued that the Judeo-Christian tradition should be taught not merely as our history or as influential or for its roles—all of which are now legal and encouraged by the U.S. Supreme Court—but as the truth about life. The textbooks now, all agree, do a bad job of presenting religion at all. Now they are supposed to make some sort of case for the Judeo-Christian tradition. So far, so good.

Which Jews, though, will sit down with which Christians to write which texts that will be satisfactory to which publisher and bought by which school board and used by which teachers? Suppose we convince the nation's four best-known Baptists to write, expecting pluralist (Jewish?) publishers to peddle their books to Mormon school boards in Utah where a stray Catholic teaches. What *consensus juris* would arise on those grounds? I keep getting stuck at the four best-known Baptists: our committee would have to satisfy the Reverends Jerry Falwell, Jesse Jackson, Harvey Cox, and the Honorable Senator Jesse Helms. What would they come up with that would better our situation?

I do not mean to trivialize the whole debate over how religion might ground the morality that, Americans believe, is necessary for the civic virtue that undergirds the *consensus juris* that gives authority to and is responsive to constitutional republican life. The great gift of the Founders, it seems to me, is to keep the religiophilosophical basis for their own constitutional activities as broad and vague and blurry as possible—and then, in the First Amendment, to prevent congressional "establishment" of religion that would lead to even the most subtle coercion—or to prohibit free exercise, which prohibition would have also been coercive.

Instead, they help legitimate what has come to be called the voluntary tradition, based on the rhetoric of persuasion. This tradition seems to me to be jeopardized today. To ask the public schools to do what the rest of society does not choose freely to do is to bring in an element of coercion that could rightfully lead to rebellion and more lawlessness. To the neoconservatives who make the argument for subtly coerced Judeo-Christianism (and, let me note, not only they do, and not all of them do), I must send an ironic jab: Most of them argue for capitalist laissez-faire free enterprise in all other areas of life. (American religion has prospered institutionally, one might note, on analogous religious grounds!) Yet, the more capitalist and free-enterprised a sphere of life is, the more legally free it is to give privilege to religion or to a particular religion, the less does it do so. Try to find explicit reference to this tradition or religion in the grants of the great foundations, which hardly notice religion. Try to find traces in prime-time television, where no law limits expression of religion but where practice and ethos exclude it. Try to discern a trace of a vestige of a remembrance of a hint of that tradition in magazine, newspaper, and especially television. Where is it in the corporate board room? On the stock market?

The answer given in all these cases to the absence is one that notes that the people who make up these spheres and entities are not less religious than the rest of the population. (In some cases I can prove that, by external measurements at least, they are more so.) Instead, American pluralism defeats them. How sell toothpaste to Mormons who might not like their representation on television? How sell feminine deodorants to Catholics who are offended by a sponsor of a program with a positive view of Mormonism? How grant funds to Baptists, with hungry Episcopalians looking on? Pluralism, diversity, and competition do us in, it is said.

So we turn to the public schools, with respect for their potential and disrespect for their burdened agenda. Instead of building up family, neighborhood, town meeting, public forum, and church and synagogue, an element in the public wants the schools to do the generating of religion behind morality behind civic virtue behind *consensus juris* behind the Constitution. And all this through a School Prayer amendment, by a minute for God, or, most boldly, by teaching distinctive Judeo-Christian (and especially Christian) doctrine as the truth about life, the instrument for discipling. To state it that way is to begin to outline difficulties behind the rhetoric of coercion.

The rhetoric of persuasion remains the grand instrument for which ''the separation of church and state,'' ''nonestablishment,'' ''free exercise,'' and the Constitution made provision. As has often been made clear, the same James Madison who opposed establishment and privilege was also for what Paul J. Weber calls "equal separation" of church and state. Such equality also means that there dare be no disability for religious individuals or groups who would like to use the public forum and political arena to advance their cause.

> *Equal separation* . . . rejects all political privilege, coercion or disability based on religious affiliation, belief or practice, or lack thereof, but guarantees to religiously motivated or affiliated individuals and organizations the same rights and privileges extended equally to other similarly situated individuals and organizations. It provides protection without privilege.[13]

On such grounds, using the rhetoric of persuasion, the Catholic bishops have a perfect right to organize against abortion or the nuclear bomb and for a "welfare" economy; the fundamentalists have an assured freedom to advance on the White House and try to get creationism taught in the schools. Instead of griping or seeking to invoke "separation of church and state" clauses, citizens have another option. Madison spelled that out when he discussed factions and sects in *Federalist Papers,* numbers 10 and 51: If one does not like the way someone organizes, one counterorganizes. In the multiplicity of the sects and interests, the republic would find its strength.

Madison and others believed that enough commonality was at the heart of the republic to allow for such diversity and to legitimate efforts to persuade. The assets remain, and they come better into view, when we try not to amend or repeal the Constitution, to overclaim "the intentions of the Founders," or to wish we could have all church-state issues fought out locally or no higher than on state levels, where establishment is easier to restore, where free exercise is easier to limit.

These assets include our shared and beloved space and our urgent time; our national memory and narrative and myth and symbol and rite and cer-

---

[13]Paul J. Weber, "James Madison and Religious Equality," *Review of Politics* 44:2 (April 1982): 168.

emony, voluntarily rehearsed; our common problems, addresses to problems, and solutions; our common Constitution and principles or propositions ("We hold these truths . . . "); and even what was better understood among the fighting Framers and Founders of 1787 than it is today: the bonds of affectivity, or, as Jefferson would have it, "affection."

There are risks in these aspirations to the expression of the common on a voluntary basis. Yet, gains made on the basis of them are more firm than are those that result from even the mildest coercion. And failures are less harmful than when establishment and privilege go awry. These are good days for debate over the religious dimensions of life in a constitutional republic. That we debate these profound themes is an outcome that, I would risk surmising, is one thing we can relate to "the intentions of the Founders."

//// Church, State, and Religious Freedom /////////////

// Robert Edgar, responder ////

I would like to begin a commentary on Martin Marty's chapter by quoting from another Martin, who spoke many years ago, whom some of us knew in person. In a book published shortly after his death, Martin Luther King said:

> We are now faced with the fact that tomorrow is today. We are confronted with the fierce urgency of *now*. In this unfolding conundrum of life and history, there is such a thing as being too late. Procrastination is still the theft of time. Life often leaves us standing, bare naked and dejected with lost opportunity. Time in the affairs of humanity does not remain at the flood, it ebbs. We may cry out desperately for time to pause in her passage, but time is deaf to every plea and rushes on. Over the bleached bones and jumbled residues of numerous civilizations will be written the pathetic words, *too late*.
>
> There is an invisible book of life that faithfully records our vigilance or our neglect. The moving finger writes, and having writ, moves on. We still have a choice today, non-violent co-existence or violent co-annihilation. This may well be mankind's last chance to choose between chaos and community.

King's words disturb the complacency we get ourselves into; they shock us out of the way of life that we were living; they force us to stop and open our minds to think. Marty has also helped us really to begin to think. He is right that one does not understand the world in only secular terms. It has been clear to me as a congressman who has served twelve years in the House of Representatives that one does not understand the world we live in unless we understand its religious dimensions. We are a people of religions, and yet, so often, we who are in the secular or the sacred, find it so fragile a discussion that we do not talk about it.

One really does not understand the world we live in if we think only in secular terms. Sometimes I get the feeling that our State Department thinks only in secular terms. How can one understand what is going on in El Salvador, Nicaragua, or Honduras, for instance, without understanding liberation theology? How can we make sense of the conflicts in the Middle East without understanding the difference between Shiite and Sunni Moslems? Our schools are so frightened to talk about religions. They do not teach it.

Marty is also right about his comments on the state. One does not understand America as a state or government without recognizing a separation of church and state (or church*es* and state*s*). But it is not a separation, as we have heard, of people of faith and institutions of government. One can buy legal advice, but one cannot buy common sense. And so the Bob Drinans and Bob Edgars who find their way into the halls of the House of Representatives, who take their faith statements and make them work on questions of world hunger, education, and literacy, are of equal value to those who come from other professions to make public laws. Yes, we should separate institutions from government, but not people of faith from institutions of government.

I was intrigued by Marty's comment about the state's being over the church. Perhaps someday all of the religious communities will find their place under the state and give it the principles and guidance and rules that could sustain its moral character. Gandhi came very close to that view when he listed the seven deadly sins: wealth without work, pleasure without conscience, knowledge without character, commerce without morality, science without humanity, worship without sacrifice, and politics without principles.

I agree with Marty that the question of real liberty is at the heart of this discussion. One comes very close to understanding the meaning of life when one understands one's own religious liberty. The church cannot uphold the state, because sometimes the state is wrong. I think of the sanctuary movement, where the church, in some instances, tried to protect those who, if they had returned to their homeland, would have faced certain death. I think of the young man in California who just recently stood in front of a train bearing munitions to Central America and got his legs chopped off—nearly the ultimate act of nonviolent yet violent civil disobedience. And I think of many of us who have been empowered by preachers who have given us a new vision, a new power. I think of the traditions of law and order that we are upholding two hundred years later. And I think that Marty is right in talking about trust and adaptability.

For over two hundred years the Constitution has shaped our lives and protected our freedom, including our religious freedom. And it is remarkable that we can gather ourselves at this moment to ask the question of church, state, and liberty. In the year 2187, I wonder, when the Constitution is four hundred years old, will the children of that generation be smart enough still to ask this question?

////Church, State, and Religious Freedom//////////////

// Edmund B. Spaeth, responder////

Professor Marty's chapter is a sweet-tempered, sunny presentation of a subject that is so often marked by anything but a sweet temper, by all sorts of bitterness and intolerance and persecution. In fact, he has given such a balanced presentation that one almost feels frustrated. I find myself asking how this wonderfully detached and learned man, who is at the same time obviously engaged very much with modern life and flow, can end his chapter by urging a tradition of voluntarism—"a rhetoric of persuasion," as he puts it. If one does not like what a group is pressing for, one should counterorganize.

I think that no one can really fault such a tradition, since it is a very wise deduction from our history. Just in passing, it seems to me that one of the most interesting aspects of Marty's chapter is how it brings out the extent to which we at this particular time have indeed changed our whole way of looking at things. We used to have established churches, and indeed the First Amendment did only provide that Congress shall make no law. We do not look at that limitation now as affecting our lives—quite to the contrary, as Marty pointed out—for the First Amendment is applicable to all states. So there has been great change, to the point where the fact that the Founding Fathers certainly had a very different philosophy than many persons do today does not control how we approach this subject. This is, quintessentially, not a problem that can be resolved by any originalist or

Framers'-intention way of looking at the problems. But I do respectfully suggest that relying on a voluntary tradition, or a rhetoric of persuasion or counterorganizing, does underestimate the passion that Santayana addressed and that Marty recognizes.

Such rhetoric will take us to a point, but only to a point. Recall the underlying premises of our Constitution, which were phrased in terms of the state of nature. Currently, the natural law of philosophy is not much in vogue in the departments of philosophy. In a sense, it may be a historical anachronism. But, it is, nevertheless, an underlying premise of our Constitution. And I think that natural law has very important implications as we approach this problem of freedom of exercise of religion and the prohibition against establishing any kind of church religion. The premise of those who drafted the Constitution was that each one of us had a bundle of natural rights, which very broadly can be referred to as the rights to life, liberty, and the pursuit of happiness. Those rights preceded government.

In the view of the Framers, the difficulty was that, left to ourselves, we are a rather nasty lot. The strong will oppress the weak and will undertake to deprive them of their natural rights. To prevent that from being done, a government is created. Now, since the only function of government is to ensure that each of us enjoys our natural rights, government is a limited creature. We, the people, give the government only as much power as it needs to enable each of us to enjoy our natural rights. All other powers we reserve to ourselves. The Bill of Rights, as Marty observes, was not adopted until four years after the Constitution was. The Bill of Rights was seen as a matter of rhetoric. As a matter of logic, it was thought to be unnecessary, because if we had only given government the limited powers needed to enable each of us to enjoy our natural rights, and if we reserve all other rights, what more does one need to say?

The answer given was that this view *can* be misunderstood, so let us say it twice. Not only should we make it plain that we are reserving all of the rights that we do not delegate, we should specify *which* of those reserved rights government may not invade. So the Bill of Rights is saying affirmatively what was implied in the Constitution itself. And, of course, one of those specific rights that must not be invaded by the government is the freedom of worship. I go here into these elementary matters because I think we have to start from there in thinking whether the rhetoric of persuasion, the voluntary tradition, will do.

The difficulty with the freedom of worship clause and the establishment clause is that one runs into the other. Marty referred indirectly to the case involving the Amish—*Wisconsin* v. *Yoder.* Now that case can be looked at, and was looked at by the Court, as a freedom of worship case. The Amish only wanted to worship as they had for many years, and that included not sending their children to school after fourteen. But the more freedom of worship one grants, the closer one comes to establishing a church. I suggest that we cannot separate the two clauses. The dichotomy is not as clear as perhaps might appear from Marty's discussion. The standard language in these cases is that there is an absolute right to *believe,* but that the right to *act* is not absolute. That distinction was made very clear in the first freedom of religion case that came before the United States Supreme Court. That case involved the question whether the Mormons were entitled, as a matter of free exercise of religion, to polygamy. The Court said, in effect, you can believe anything, but you cannot act as you wish, at least not absolutely. There will have to be some limits. And the Court, in the course of its opinion, asked the rhetorical question, Would anyone suppose that we would, in the name of freedom of religion, tolerate human sacrifice? Cases have continued to press this theme.

What does one do if, under the freedom of religion, somebody says, ''I don't want my child to have a blood transfusion'' or ''I insist upon handling snakes'' or ''I insist upon taking hallucinogenics'' or, as in a case that is currently under litigation in New York, ''we insist upon ritual sacrifice of animals.'' Those activities all are subject to state regulation. What is the standard to be applied as to whether the state may forbid the ritual sacrifice of animals by invoking health laws, or may forbid the handling of poisonous snakes? Or consider a case that was decided recently by the Court, involving this matter of creationism and human secularism. What does one do when one group insists that an institution is teaching something that they denominate is a religion (namely, human secularism) and is not giving equal attention to something they call a science (namely, creationism)?

With respect, I suggest that you cannot simply rely upon persuasion or counterorganization. There will come a point where the state will have to intervene. Under our constitutional system, the moment one says, it is all very well to have the government protect the natural rights of each of us, then the question arises, suppose the government does not, or suppose the government goes too far? Who is to say or define what may or may not be done? Who is to say whether an intrusion by the government oversteps the mark, or violates our desire to worship as we wish, or so supports some group who wishes to worship that it verges on establishing a church? The answer that we gave, of course, was that the courts should do it.

I fully agree with Marty that some of the most exciting cases that come before the courts each term are the cases involving the free exercise and establishment clauses. They are exciting because of the passions that are kindled by the litigants, the depth of the feelings, and this yearning for some sort of consensus. The courts find themselves in an agonizing position because an adjudication must be made. An adjustment of these demands must be made in nonreligious terms, which is a very difficult thing to do. And it is consistent, I suggest, with the original impulse underlying the assumption of our Constitution that each one of us must be allowed to develop our own view of life, as long as our beliefs do not involve us in conduct that deprives others. And there is no firm line that can be drawn.

Sometimes in the law you can see a line of cases developing that seem to be growing out of each other—for example, the cases involving the interstate commerce clause, where one sees courts developing the reach of the Congress in their ability to regulate commerce among the states. What is encompassed in the notion of commerce? How direct, how indirect can the regulation be? Such cases do not go in a straight line. They zigzag a bit, but there is growth.

We do not find such growth, however, with the cases involving the freedom of religion and establishment clauses. We find instead one agonized balancing act after the other. May the state grant tuition credits?

Well, yes, if everyone gets them, perhaps. But may the state give the money to the schools directly? Well, no. Why not? And how far? And may the state put up a crèche on a public square?

As he read the crèche case, Justice Black dissented, in quite an eloquent dissent. The argument that persuaded the 5-4 majority was, essentially, "Don't take it so seriously." There are lots of other Santa Clauses and various decorations of the holiday season; it is all a matter of holiday festivity and feeling, and we have done that sort of thing for a long time. The dissenters said, "You *must* take such symbols seriously. When you put up only the crèche, what does that say to people who are not Christians? Are you excluding them, or do they feel excluded? You have not put up everything, you have only one symbol." Justice Black, in his separate opinion, said the only way the majority can stand by its decision is to reduce this central symbol of Christianity to just a sort of commercial display. And that is a very unsatisfactory decision. And not one, I think, we can have much confidence in as a precedent.

Without sounding gloomy, then, I must say that, for myself, I foresee only continued struggling, probably of continued intensity. I do not see a resolution of it by counterorganization or persuasion, and I fear that the resolutions will be continued to be made in terms of litigation that ends up before the Supreme Court. The Supreme Court, I fear, will continue to make decisions that will be very difficult to reconcile. They will be a matter of gradation, of balancing—essentially of an intuitive feeling. There cannot be any wall of separation—indeed, it is a wavering line. At this point, we think it has wavered a little too far. I think, though, that the spirit of toleration, accommodation, and historical sense that inform Marty's chapter will be an enormous resource. And, indeed, our differences are by no means as severe as they were earlier in Western civilization. But as much as that contribution will be valued, in the end, I expect, we will have to resort—as we have so often—to constitutional adjudication. Such an answer will continue to be uncertain and satisfactory to some, and not satisfactory to others.

//// Church, State, and Religious Freedom //////////

// Jacqueline G. Wexler, responder////

I agree with Dr. Marty on main things, I was particularly relieved that he dissented from a notion of a wall and chose rather a line. I guess I would go further and think of it as an arena, or a zone.

Characteristic of the Constitution is the tension of powers among the three forms of government. But then it always goes back to "We, the people." And we, the people, in that preamble, were challenged to try to create a *more* perfect union (not a perfect one; they were too smart for that), to establish domestic tranquility, and to establish justice. Given all those conjoint responsibilities, they recognized, at least in a beginning way, that they were already a very pluralistic people.

I was intrigued with Marty's distinction between subordinancy and subserviency. I like it a lot, because I have, for many years, tried to make a fundamental distinction between regulatory authority and teaching authority. Obviously, governmental authority, whether it is the mother and father presiding over young children in a home or, indeed, a federal government, is regulatory authority. It sets up a series of regulations that have sanctions if we do not follow them. But teaching authority is quite different. It is subservient to regulatory authority in legal senses, but I would argue that it is often *above* regulatory authority in its ability to inform the intelligence and form the conscience. And so, to the degree that I am a woman of faith, it is because I have heard and ingested the teaching and made it my own.

Now, the teaching authorities to "we, the people" are religious, political, philosophical, ethical, and perhaps many others. They are in the
memory genes of our faith traditions, whether those faiths are sacred or
secular or both. They are in the environment around us, and in a pluralistic society, those teaching sources are often contradictory. And so,
in my young life, in conversations with persons who called themselves
atheistic scientists, I have said that dogmatic theists and dogmatic atheists are fraternal twins. And agnostics and persons of faith are fraternal
twins. And I, from the memory genes in my faith tradition, like John of
the Cross and Teresa of Ávila, say: I believe, I believe, I believe; O God,
help my unbelief. And you, as a person of science say: I see no evidence, I see no evidence, I see no evidence—but I wonder. And we share
with each other because we have a conjoint way of looking at the world.
But the dogmatists cannot share with each other or with any of us, if to
be dogmatic means there is an absolutist position.

A few weeks before this forum, I was privileged to stand on a stage
here in Philadelphia and to present signatures to the chief justice. I was
intrigued with his very brief remarks. The one thing he seized upon was
that the Founders forever broke tradition with the divine right of kings.
And then, in the middle of the bell ringing, that wonderful old man on
his eightieth birthday (many of whose decisions I do not agree with),
ringing the bell with the children and with me in a marvelous moment
of my life, said, "Let's give it to the children, Jacqueline. They are the
future." And we took our hands off the bell, and they rang it. That is
secular and sacred faith—to give it to the children. They are the future.
To teach authoritatively, not absolutely; to put some regulations in it,
but then to let the children go.

I would argue that that kind of religion is really only evolving. Because the two hundred years of this republic is the first experiment of
any religion living in a pluralistic democracy in which religion is always
subservient in the regulatory sense. And it is therefore reduced or ex-
alted—and I would like to think the second—depending on our teaching
authority.

Now let me take another step. Particularly in this century, we are
trying to understand mutuality instead of patriarchy; we, as people, are

trying to understand differential dignity rather than hierarchical dignity. As a people in the Christian church under John XXIII and Vatican II, for the first time we came to terms with *two* covenants. Not the (common) Judeo-Christian traditions, but the Jewish and Christian covenants. This insight says boldly and forthrightly that God, whoever he/she is, made a covenant with one people that is differential from the covenant that he/she made with another people. Both covenants ring true, and one can assert the other. If God be God and is the common parent of us all, then how could he/she have meant his/her Testaments to have divided us from one another to perpetrate programs and religious wars on one another?

And if there is a person, a presence, a spirit, we call God, perhaps we are on the dawn of time in the tiny learning curve of two hundred years from centuries of tribal cultures who believed in the divine right of kings. (And how could one believe in such a ''right'' unless one had convinced oneself and everybody else that one had the pipeline, and the only pipeline?) But maybe we are at the dawn of a kind of humble courage that says, I can celebrate my particularity—and that is my covenant. But my covenantal relationship with God does not depend on the lesser dignity or the indignity of another.

If such courage and respect is a possibility (and I hope and, to some degree, believe it is), then the free cooperation is a perpetual compromise. As a little girl raised in parochial school, who learned her Latin well, I have always been fascinated with such words. *Com-promise* means ''to have promise with''—not to water down. In that preamble, when they said, ''We, the people, in order to form a more perfect union, to establish tranquility,'' maybe it was to fill that promise with.

Finally, I would argue that the voluntary tradition, the rhetoric of persuasion, is clearly in the whole First Amendment. The First Amendment, in a single sentence, guarantees us freedom from established religion, provides freedom of worship, and in a coordinate, rhetorical structure, gives us freedom of speech and freedom of assembly. And so I cannot understand how we can chain the Bibles to the stools in the school. One can take away established religion but of course cannot coerce worship. And the courts have agreed conclusively that one cannot coerce worship in public schools, because our schools have required attendance laws. But if we are going to raise up young children to participate and lead us—we, the people—in the most pluralistic democracy the world has seen, how can we do that without trying to form teachers who might understand in some secular/sacred sense what David Hartman has called "a theology of particularity"; who can communicate to little kids that there are no number one, number two, and number three daughters and sons. But only number ones. As an educator, I believe that we have to take very tiny steps, but I would argue that we of religious faith—if it is faith and not binding—have got to trust one another enough to begin to do so. How can one teach Anne Frank in the schools without teaching Jewish faith? How can one teach Martin Luther King without teaching Christian faith? How can one teach Gandhi in the schools without teaching his faith? And on and on and on.

I do not think it is simple. I think it has to be bite sized. I think we have to have enormous faith and humility, which I would suggest is always part of faith. And then we must depend on that other tension of powers that is regulatory and know that we, the people, inform the legislators and elect the presidents and, to some degree, even educate those who will be the Supreme Court justices when the children are the future.

Doctrine of Accommodation
and the Religious Clauses
of the Constitution

/// Arlin M. Adams////

In my humble opinion, two of the great gifts of the United States to the world have been the Constitution, including the Bill of Rights, and the concept of freedom of religion (freedom of conscience to worship as one will), with the concomitant right of separation of church and states. Those particular rights come about as a result of the First Amendment to the Constitution and that portion of the First Amendment that is generally referred to as "the religion clauses": "Congress shall make no law respecting an establishment of religion, or prohibiting the free exercise thereof." That is all there is. It has magnificent cadence and balance. It was ratified in 1791, and those clauses were presumed to be a cohesive and harmonious protection of the rights I have just mentioned. They excited very little attention for more than a century. But in the twentieth century the story was different. There has been an explosion of cases involving both of these clauses. And there has been a great deal of jurisprudence and a great deal of writing. A book that I have been working on for a long time is now in excess of two volumes.

Recently, Chief Justice Rehnquist lamented that these clauses have created a kind of Scylla and Charybdis, which, to me, evokes images of Ulysses' perilous journey through the Strait of Messina. The image implies that, if the monster of establishment clause doctrine does not trap the unwary sailor, then the world full of free exercise will. In comparing the jurisprudence of the clauses to Scylla and Charybdis, the chief justice criticizes much of his own Court's doctrine, because the Court has given a very broad reading to both the clauses. He maintains they should have a narrow reading so that one will not overlap the other, so that they will not overwhelm the navigator. I would like to address here the width and depth of the passage between those two visual images that the chief justice has posed. The two clauses I would prefer to compare to beacons, which together can enlighten our understanding of the practice of religion in a pluralistic society.

The space between the clauses that allows the government voluntarily to accommodate the religious beliefs of its citizens has been commonly referred to as "the permissible zone of accommodation." An accommodation, therefore, respects the pluralism of our people without undermining the concept of establishment. The zone between the clauses has been the subject of great commentary, but also of a great deal of controversy. The Supreme Court has already recognized that a permissible zone exists in the gray area between government actions that violate the establishment clause and individual religious rights that the free exercise clause says may not be dictated or burdened by the government.

The issue of such a zone goes back to about thirty-five years ago in a rather famous case, *Zorach* v. *Clauson,* which involved "release time" in New York City. Justice Douglas upheld a program that permitted public school children to be released about an hour before the usual time in order to go to church or religious education, if that is what they wanted to do. He said that it did not violate the establishment clause because it accommodated, rather than advanced, religion.

Permissible accommodation is an area of allowable government deference to the religious requirements of our society. But this kind of *voluntary* accommodation should not be confused with references to accommodation that may be *required* by the free exercise clause. When Chief Justice Burger spoke in the case of *Lynch* v. *Donnelly* the famous crèche case in Rhode Island, he talked about an affirmative mandate to accommodate, which was imposed on government by the free exercise guarantee. He was not talking about the type of accommodation that we are talking about today. He was referring to the doctrine that, if a free exercise right has been determined to have been infringed, then the government must accommodate that right, unless there is a compelling and narrowly tailored state interest. I return later to this issue.

Also distinguishable from the permissible accommodation that we talk about today is government action that actually abridges the establishment clause. That is frequently referred to as forbidden or impermissible accommodation. *Forbidden accommodation* is a term describing governmental action that has gone beyond the bounds of allowable deference to religious expression and belief and that, instead, actually endorses a particular religion. We thus have to distinguish the permissible from the mandatory and the disallowed.

When it was announced, *Zorach* was quite a controversial decision, mainly because, only four years earlier in the *McCollum* case, the Court had said one cannot release children from a public school in order to attend prayer or worship services if those services are conducted on the premises of the school. In order to get around this decision, *Zorach* said that the services will be conducted off the premises of the school, the children being permitted to go to their local church or wherever they want to conduct their prayer services.

For most of its history, the accommodation theory has been favored by so-called moderates. In using the term *moderate,* I take it to mean those who believe that, while religion has a vital role in American life and should not be burdened by excessive intrusion and governmentally imposed liabilities, the establishment clause must, nonetheless, be enforced and be enforced diligently. Recently, some writers have insisted that the accommodation doctrine should be expanded—and expanded significantly—beyond its traditionally rather narrow scope. They think that, if one has too much accommodation, one gradually erodes the concept of nonestablishment. I do not believe that the history of the clauses or case law supports that concern or that position.

When properly applied, the accommodation doctrine is a helpful analytical tool that resolves much of the tension between the two clauses.

Because accommodation demands a careful balance between antiestablishment and the free exercise principles, we have to recognize that light from both clauses is vital to a safe passage between the twin guardians; otherwise, we can compromise our fundamental mandates.

I hasten to suggest that we ought to limit accommodation to those situations in which the danger of establishment would be remote. Furthermore, the religious interest accommodated by government action must be related to the rights protected by the free exercise clause. In other words, an accommodation should relieve a governmentally imposed burden on religious conduct. But accommodation must not be confused with free exercise. For not all burdens on religion entitle a religious believer to constitutionally impelled relief.

Where there has been a challenge to government action on the ground that it infringes upon religious belief, the courts must first determine whether it removes a burden that has been placed on that religious belief by the government's own regulation. If the court perceives it that way, then I suggest that the accommodation would not be violating the establishment clause. Second, the courts should determine whether the governmentally imposed burden would entitle the plaintiff to free exercise relief. If so, the removal of the burden is, in reality, a legislative interpretation of constitutional requirements and is really not a voluntary accommodation. A little later I will give you some examples, because this is rather arcane material. But the test is really a two-prong test: Do we have a governmentally imposed burden on religious exercise, and is the believer to be entitled to relief?

In order to see this picture a little more clearly, we ought to go back to the original drafting in 1791. At that time, the establishment and free exercise clauses were intended, I believe, to have a much more narrow sweep than they have today. The dramatic expansion of the federal government and the application of the clauses to the states through a doctrine known as ''incorporation'' combine to extend their reach into areas that were never contemplated by the drafters and our Founding Fathers.

It is interesting to see what James Madison, the drafter of these clauses, actually had in mind. He said, ''The civil rights of none shall be abridged on account of religious belief or worship, nor shall any national religion be established, nor shall the full and equal rights of conscience be in any manner or on any pretext infringed.'' Madison explained the meaning of the proposal as providing that Congress should not establish a religion. And that really was the big question back in those days. The Anglicans in Virginia were worried that the Congregationalists in Massachusetts would establish their religion—that it would be the national religion in the United States. The Congregationalists were, in turn, worried that Virginia, the largest state in the Union, would establish their religion, and we would have a repeat in this country of what they had gone through in Great Britain. But there is no doubt that the representatives to the Constitutional Convention did not wish to abolish religion altogether. Their primary purpose was to preclude the imposition of a federal religion. The wording eventually adopted makes clear the exclusively federal application of what they were concerned with. They specified that *Congress* shall make no law respecting an establishment of religion. The clause—intentionally—said nothing about the states.

The Framers were completely satisfied with what they had. The Congregational religion was at that time the established religion in Massachusetts; even in Virginia, the Anglican religion was still pretty much an established religion. We had established religions in the United States as late as 1833. And some of you might wonder how that could be. What about the Constitution? The Constitution referred to Congress: ''*Congress* shall make no law.'' In the early 1800s, there was some question whether the Bill of Rights was applicable to the states. John Marshall decided that matter with his colleagues on the court. In the famous case of *Baron* v. *Baltimore,* the Court decided that the Bill of Rights literally was to be applied only to the federal government; it starts with the word *Congress.* And in the *Permoli* take note case, involving Roman Catholics, Marshall repeated his position.

But in the United States there were great feelings about slavery and our fellow citizens in the South. The South wanted to have slavery and advanced the idea of states' rights. People in the North who did not want slavery advanced the idea of a strong federal government. And the Civil War was fought.

As a result of the Civil War and public sentiment, there was a series of Civil War amendments—the Thirteenth, Fourteenth, and Fifteenth amendments. These amendments were applicable to the states, and that was one of the big battles of the 1800s in the United States. The Fourteenth Amendment contains, among other things, the due process clause. Now, it says "due process" or "equal protection." It does not mention religion or the right of free speech or the free press or things like that. Over a considerable period of time, primarily in the early 1900s, the Supreme Court gradually adopted a doctrine that was known as "the doctrine of incorporation," which said, in effect, that the Bill of Rights was now made applicable to the states through the passage of the Fourteenth Amendment and the due process and equal protection clauses. This interpretation was a long time in coming, and it took a lot of cases. Finally, in 1940 and 1947, the Supreme Court announced two very important decisions: *Cantwell* and *Everson*. And those decisions stated flatly that the free exercise clause and the establishment clause would now be applicable to the states. As you might guess, the flood of litigation was under way.

The litigation was really augmented by the fact that the federal government was now doing more things in the social welfare field—health, education, and things like that. More than in the past, then, what the government was doing was going to collide with what individuals perceived to be their rights, whether they were civil rights, political rights, or religious rights.

The *Everson* case, in 1947, which announced that the establishment would now be applicable to the states, was a busing case in New Jersey. New Jersey legislature said that the local school districts could reimburse parents who sent children to parochial schools. And immediately, there was a big hubbub over in Mount Holly, and people said, "That's establishing a religion." That case eventually went to the Supreme Court of the United States. In a 5-4 decision, the Court held that the busing did not quite establish a religion because there is a social-welfare basis for sending poor children to school without running the risk that they will be hit in an automobile accident. This case is interesting because it shows how important one vote can be. Justice Douglas cast the deciding vote in *Everson,* but three years later in *Zorach* he effectively admitted that he had earlier made a mistake. If Douglas had not voted as he did in *Everson,* most of the current tension in this area and most of the cases never would have come about. The *Everson* case really started most of what we are now considering.

As these cases unfolded, it soon became apparent to the Supreme Court and to the scholars that there was a certain amount of tension between these two clauses. If the courts give each person the right of free exercise, then the government (either federal or state) might begin establishing religion. The most important case that will illustrate this tension is the *Walz,* case, which challenged New York's exemption of all church property from real estate taxes. All the states in fact exempt church property and have done so from time immemorial in the United States. Mr. Walz decided that he was going to test that question. So he bought a little piece of property on Staten Island, filed a lawsuit, and, claiming that granting of exemptions to all of these churches really establishes a religion, asked the courts to strike down these exemptions.

The case went to the Supreme Court, and Chief Justice Berger recognized (and this was really the first time that the Supreme Court or any of the justices recognized) that there was this tension and that, to some extent, Walz was right. If the courts give a church an exemption from all taxes, they certainly are helping to establish religion. But Chief Justice Berger said there has to be some sort of accommodation. There is a clash here, but if one takes each of these clauses to their absolute extreme, they would clash head on. And in this case, there is a reason to accommodate the free exercise of religion because, if the courts began burdening church property and religious property with taxes, they would effectively close down a considerable number of churches and religious establishments because they could not afford the taxation. The government therefore ought to accommodate that situation. It is not establishing a religion, because all religious organizations—Episcopalian, Mohammedan, whatever—would have the same benefit. At the same time, this exemption properly applies to all nonprofit corporations (YMCAs, YMHAs, universities, and so forth).

Strangely enough, Justice Douglas, who was the author of the *Zorach* opinion, which first recognized accommodations, strongly dissented. He argued that the surest way to establish religion in the United States is to give it a financial benefit. Nothing could be of greater financial benefit than tax exemption. In his footnotes he added up all the advantages that churches had received from tax exemption and found that it goes into the millions and billions of dollars. But for me the case is mainly important as establishing this doctrine of accommodation. Chief Justice Berger did not think it through as completely as some of the judges have done today, but he was at the so-called cutting edge.

This case, however, did pose a serious question for the scholars. When do we say that something is accommodated? When is it established? When is it not established? Professor Kurland at the University of Chicago said that the keynote has to be neutrality: "Religion may not be used as a basis for classification for purposes of governmental action, whether that action be the conferring of rights or privileges or the imposition of duties or obligations." That became a well known but debated proposition. If one follows Kurland's suggestion, one would begin cutting back on religious freedoms and religious opportunities.

A second approach was by Professor Tribe. According to Tribe, we ought to have two different definitions of religion (although religion is used in the Constitution only once). He said that we ought to favor free exercise and that establishment should take a second place. Justice O'-Connor addressed this tension quite recently in the case *Wallace* v. *Jaffree,* which is one of the "moment of silence" cases.

In 1963, the Supreme Court struck down prayer in school. Some people thought it would be a good idea to get around that decision for the benefit of kids who do wish to pray and tell them, in effect, "You don't have to pray; you can sit there quietly for a minute, and if you want to pray silently, you may." This particular statute happened to be struck down for some extraneous reasons. But in the course of the opinion, Justice O'Connor said the solution to the conflict between the clauses lies not in neutrality but rather in identifying workable limits to the government's license to promote the free exercise of religion. And then she picked up a phrase that Berger had used in the *Walz* case when he said, "There has to be some play in the joints." I think she has the right approach to this very difficult problem. We are not talking about compulsion or coercion or about establishing religions or any particular religion or church. We are talking about permitting the government to remove a particular burden if the burden that it has incidentally imposed happens to strike across someone's religious beliefs or conscience.

A very good example is the Braunfeld case, which arose in Philadelphia involving Sunday closing. An orthodox Jew in South Philadelphia brought a lawsuit under the free exercise clause, claiming that, since he had to close his business on both Saturday and Sunday, he would go bankrupt.

The Supreme Court, in a 5-4 decision, voted against him. Now, would it have established a religion if the state legislature had said that this law was not applicable for someone who does not ordinarily observe Sundays? Muhammedans observe Friday. Jews and Seventh-Day Adventists observe Saturday. It should not be applicable to them if there is a bona fide belief. That allowance would be an accommodation, in my way of thinking, because it would not establish a religion. It merely lifts the restriction that the state legislature has imposed that everyone should cease work on Sunday. I guess I am suggesting that, if the danger of establishment is somewhat remote or attenuated and there is a free exercise basis for lifting the exemption, then it is justified.

A rather famous case in the Supreme Court in 1986 called *Amos* involved the Mormons. Under the Equal Rights amendment, one cannot discharge an employee in a discriminatory fashion but must have a valid reason. The Mormons adopted a rule that they wanted only Mormons to be employed in their churches and in their other religious facilities. Although I am not suggesting that it is a good rule, it is a rule borne out of their religious convictions. And they discharged an employee named Amos who did not follow the Mormon religion. The question was whether the provision in Article 7 in the Civil Rights Act established a religion. The provision permitted churches, if they saw fit, to discharge persons who did not follow their particular religion. In a very close case, the Supreme Court said no, the accommodation in the act is reasonable. It does not establish any religion, because it applies to all religions. It is not discriminatory.

Now there is a certain amount of danger in allowing such dismissals. If it is done too frequently for the majority religions, then some of the minority religions can suffer. I have only a stock answer for that concern: "It's a legitimate inquiry." That is why we need courts, why we need justices on the Supreme Court and judges on the other courts who can exercise common sense and be sensitive to the situation. There are no absolute answers to many of these very difficult problems. Eventually they get down to a question of degree. Does it make sense? Does it represent what the Founding Fathers had in mind? And does it represent good sense in view of the evolution of the country? There are no stock answers. Anyone who suggests that there are, either by trying to divine the intent of James Madison or Thomas Jefferson or by appealing to some modern-day consensus, I think is not being realistic.

It has been well established that the United States government could have a draft conscription law that would not grant any exemptions at all. The reason is that the need to defend the country is so great, that, even though such a law would cut across the religious convictions of many persons (Quakers, for example, who feel very strongly about not participating in controversies of that sort), it would be justified. Such a law was actually passed in 1917. Under such a law today, a Quaker could well show up at the draft board and object, "I want to do my duty, but I don't participate in armed conflict." The draft board chairman would have to answer, "I'm very sympathetic, but I can't accommodate you—that would be an establishment of religion; I would be favoring your religion." That answer perhaps would be strict logic, but I suggest it would not be common sense. It would not represent the viewpoint of the majority of people of this country. And I would see absolutely nothing wrong with accommodating the views of such persons who were conscientious objectors from a general law such as that. This is a good illustration of a permissible accommodation. It respects the religious right of the applicant. He does not quite have a free exercise right, because of the overarching importance of conscription, but I see no reason at all why the government could not create a permissible accommodation in this case.

////Accommodation and the Religious Clauses////

// Robert L. DeWitt, responder////

Judge Adams has plotted a course to guide those concerned with the interpretation of the religion clauses of the First Amendment. My comments here attempt to underscore some of the realities of religion that make his topic so crucial to American life.

The circumstance of religion in the thirteen colonies following the War of Independence was indeed unusual, if not unique. Perhaps never before had groups of such various religious persuasions settled into such a compact, new community as the colonies had become. It was appropriate—indeed, perhaps necessary—that the constitutional approach to that circumstance was similarly unique. The intention of the Framers of the Constitution was not so much to create a settlement of the question of religion as to establish a stance toward the question that would be viable for an indefinite future. How well they did depends in no small measure on how well we do.

This is not an easy task, because circumstances change. Though religion is, in part, the efforts of humans to deal with things eternal, those dealings are nevertheless done in time, in history. Religion thus has a history, it is in a state of flux, and it is subject to change. We can clearly see some basic changes that have occurred since the ratification of the Constitution. For example, one of the paramount threats that the Framers were concerned to guard against was the establishment of a state religion. Their vivid awareness of certain established religions in Europe made this possibility something for them to avoid carefully. (I note with some unease that a concerted effort to establish the Anglican episcopacy in the colonies was in some modest measure a contributing factor to the Revolution!) Actually, an establishment in the new nation was probably a historical impossibility, given the diversity of religious orientation from one colony to another. The Framers could be said to have made virtue of a necessity. As one contemplates contemporary America, it would seem equally remote that any one religious group could be established nationally today. This circumstance, however, could change. The Romans, during the early years of the reign of Constantine, would probably also have said they were in no jeopardy of an established religion. Eternal vigilance is the price of freedom from a religious establishment.

When we consider the second clause of the religion statement in the First Amendment, we again see that history has not ignored us, but that we, as a nation, have been swept along in its swirling, turbulent unpredictability. Congress, that clause states, is to make no law prohibiting the free exercise of religion. The religious regimes of some of the colonies, glad though they were to be free of the religious oppressions of Europe, nevertheless displayed a hostility toward deviation from their own religious norms, which showed they had learned well from the Old World the lesson of intolerance. The drafters of the Constitution set their faces against this tendency and ran up the flag of religious tolerance. The application of the religion clauses to the several states, through incorporation by the Fourteenth Amendment, was still a century and a half away. But the course had been set. The national posture had been declared.

But what a difference between the limited number of religious groupings known to the Constitutional Convention and the array that confronts us today! It has been said of the Roman Empire in the first century, "Two soothsayers could not meet in the streets of Rome without laughing in each other's faces." There was a spiritual vacuum abroad in the empire, and cults and charlatans were filling the void. Similarly, our years, too, have been lived out in an era when old landmarks have been blurred, when verities long thought to be eternal have been challenged or discarded, when traditional faith has been overwhelmed by doubt and skepticism. We have slipped our moorings and find ourselves adrift in unknown waters, with no clearly discerned destination or future after this life. Most of us are well educated and sophisticated in the ways of *this* world, born and bred in the manner of modernity. But we find ourselves facing the "Last Things" of this existence with no chart, no knowledge, no experience, no assurance. Consequently, our world today, like the first-century Roman Empire, is a hothouse, extremely conducive to the growth of every plant (and weed) of thought, feeling, aspiration, and desperation that grows in the lush soil of the human heart.

There was probably no religious group in the colonies that every member of the Constitutional Convention could not name and describe. Today, however, how familiar are we with the more than three hundred different denominations that have taken root in our soil? Not to mention the myriad cults, electronic churches, and syncretistic movements of Eastern origin that gather their faithful. As late as four years before his death, Thomas Jefferson stated, "I confidently expect that the present generation will see Unitarianism become the general religion of the United States." It is clear that the religious scene we survey today is vastly different from that either seen or anticipated by the writers of the Constitution. Today there is a greatly increased crowding and jostling on the stage of religion.

What is this religious factor in human life that has been with us throughout history? Each of us can answer that question only for oneself, for the religious instinct lies deeply embedded in the heart and mind and soul of every human. It can be affirmed or denied. It can take many forms of expression, as the history of religions makes clear. But there it is, an inevitable part of being human. For it arises from our being perhaps the only creatures on earth who are aware of our finitude—that is to say, who can contemplate our own death. We are thus, throughout our life, acutely aware of our vulnerability. Consequently, an inevitable anxiety accompanies us throughout all the days of our years. It may be concealed by busyness, obscured by the seeking of pleasures and novelties. Or it may become obsessively compulsive and express itself in one or another of the religious psychoses with which psychologists are familiar. But either of these extremes is only an exaggeration of the normal human circumstance. Such questions as Why am I here? From whence do I come? What is my destiny? may receive answers as various as those given by the atheist, the skeptic, the agnostic, or the theist. But the questions are unavoidable. And they are religious questions.

Adams quoted Justice Douglas's statement that "we are a religious people whose institutions presuppose a Supreme Being." James Madison, two years before the ratification of the Constitution, put it even more strongly. In his famous "Memorial and Remonstrance against Religious Assessments," Madison said, "Before any man can be considered as a member of Civil Society, he must be considered as a subject of the Governor of the Universe. . . . Every man who becomes a member of any particular Civil Society must do it with a saving of his allegiance to the Universal Sovereign." Now, this is strong language. It is the religious basis and justification for civil disobedience. Yet, reflect for a moment that there are something in the neighborhood of 150,000,000 church members of various denominations in the United States. According to their creeds and confessions, the words of Madison ring true, because as seen by the eyes of theistic faith, we on this earth live in a theocracy. Ancient Israel had it right: "The earth is the Lord's, and the fulness thereof; the world, and they that dwell therein." The dichotomy of sacred and secular is a this-worldly perception and arrangement. It seems necessary to the ordering of life in this world; but though perhaps necessary, it is provisional. The ultimate reality is sacred.

But that truth, on the one hand, and conflicting claims and approaches to that truth, on the other hand, produced the dilemma confronting the Framers of the Constitution and continue to beset those who are called to interpret that Constitution. Brotherly love has often been lacking in the encounters between religious groups, each of which professed to believe that there is one God and that all people are God's children. Despite this daunting fact, there have been giants of the faith in all generations who have seen the issue clearly. One such was Augustine of Hippo. He wrote a tract around the year A.D. 400 against a group that, to his thinking, was heretical. To that group he wrote:

> Let those be angry with you who do not know with how great toil truth is attained, or how difficult it is to avoid mistakes. . . . Let those be

> angry with you who do not know what sighs and tears are needed if the real God is to be known—even in the tiniest degree. But for me to be angry with you, is utterly impossible. . . . But in order that neither may you be angry with me, I must beg this one favour of you. Let us, on both sides, lay aside all arrogance. Let us not, on either side, claim that we have already discovered the truth. Let us seek it together.

It would be hard to find a more cogent and impassioned plea for the free exercise of religion than those words of Augustine. We must each and all be free to pursue that search for God. We must be free both from the harassments of other seekers and also from restraints imposed upon us by the body politic. The religious quest, said the Framers of the Constitution—and so say our own hearts—is to be free and unfettered.

In much of our thinking and discussing concerning the free exercise of religion, there is the unspoken assumption that religion is a purely private affair, a purely personal matter ''between a person and that person's God,'' as we say. But that individual is not an abstraction, an isolated entity. That person, you and I, are known and know ourselves only in context. And that context is community. To a frightening degree, our perceptions of ourselves, of others, of our world, of our past, present and future, and even of our God are conditioned critically and crucially by our life-in-community, by our families, neighborhoods, schools, governments, and free associations that we encounter in that human community. Any valid religion must see the entire sweep of that social context as its proper arena, as its abiding concern. There is a story of a prison in nineteenth-century Scotland that had a rule concerning the visiting of prisoners by the pastors of the churches from which they came. That rule forbade the pastor to speak with the prisoner concerning his crime, his life in prison, his family, his prior life, or his community. He was only to speak with the prisoner concerning ''spiritual matters''! With those other topics embargoed, there was not much, if anything, left of that prisoner to minister to. He was no longer a human being, just an abstraction.

True religion has to do with life in all its embodiments and involvements, in all its grandeur and its misery. True religion has to do with how one relates to the fatherless and the widow, the poor and the outcasts, with the issues of public policy and international peace, of saving this planet in order to save the people. A prayer familiar in my communion begins with the invocation "O God, with whom nothing is small that touches thy glory or the welfare of thy people. . . . " That puts it correctly. If one is to relate to God, one must relate to the concerns of God. And to God, the family of humankind is no small thing. It is *God's* family. The recent pastoral letters issued by the National Council of Catholic Bishops on the nuclear threat and on the American economy are not intrusions into fields where the bishops have no business. As church leaders, that *is* their business, and they would be derelict were they to neglect such issues that touch so heavily on the welfare of their people.

The Church of England some decades ago had a man as dean of Canterbury Cathedral who was very outspoken on international affairs and whose views were well to the left of the church at large, so much so that he was popularly known as "The Red Dean of Canterbury." Rightly or wrongly, he proved an embarrassment to the church. The archbishop of Canterbury was asked once why he did not remove the dean. He replied, "On this island we have a long tradition of freedom. We value freedom very highly. Now, the Red Dean is a high price to pay for that freedom; but we think it is worth it!"

In the 127th Psalm we find the familiar words "Except the Lord build the house, they labor in vain that build it: except the Lord keep the city, the watchman waketh but in vain." The free exercise clause of the First Amendment is the constitutional channel that provides for the Supreme Governor of the universe access to our nation's affairs. Doubtless there are, apart from the Constitution, an infinite number of other access points available to that Governor! But this country is much the richer for the contributions to national debates on affairs of state that have come from those who saw as their religious duty the obligation to attempt to influence our national life in accordance with their deeply held religious convictions.

Because of the foregoing considerations, it seems to me that the principle of accommodation is crucial to the interpretation of the Constitution. I am grateful to Judge Adams for his practical suggestions concerning a more commodious accommodation. And if such accommodation is difficult to accomplish, as he has also suggested, I would invoke a Spanish proverb: ''Wayfarer, there is no way to go. One makes the way by going.''

My own religious odyssey perhaps illustrates the complexities that beset the United States Supreme Court, or an appeals judge like Judge Adams, or a high court judge in a state like New Hampshire. I was raised originally as a Presbyterian, though I went to a Quaker school. In the summer I went to a Baptist Vacation Bible school, and I am now an Episcopalian. Such a personal history shows, in just one person, the tremendous diversity that we have and the problems that judges have in trying to balance between the various clauses and especially those in the First Amendment.

Consider some historical information, which will put things in context. The countries that settled North America—Spain, England, France, and Holland—all had established churches, and so each of the colonies came with the background of established churches in their countries of origin. By the time of the end of the colonial period, the mosaic was quite a bit different. There were 700 Congregational parishes in the U.S.; 400 or 500 each of Presbyterian, Anglican, and Baptist; 200 to 250 Quaker, Lutheran, and German Reformed; and about 60 Roman Catholic. And in Pennsylvania and in some other areas, there were Mennonites, Schwenkfelders, Amish, and so forth.

Now, how would one ever establish a church with such diversity, even back then? There were four colonies that did not have established churches—Rhode Island, which was the hard-line separationist colony; Pennsylvania, which, of course, had a little bit of everything from Quaker to various German sects to Anglican and Presbyterian; and New Jersey and Delaware. The Mid-Atlantic states probably also had the most diverse numbers of religious congregations. They had more than the typical Baptist-Anglican South and the Congregational North.

Judge Adams also mentioned that we had established churches in the other colonies. In 1816, for instance, New Hampshire dropped its established church and yet, interestingly enough, not until 1877 did the New Hampshire State Constitution drop the requirement that one must be a Protestant to serve in the legislature. In Massachusetts, church and state were separated in 1833. And not until 1844 did New Jersey give full civil rights to non-Protestants.

In 1776, then, we had the Declaration of Independence, which says that we are endowed by our Creator (capital *C*) with certain inalienable rights, including life, liberty, and property. The government was instituted, the Declaration said, to secure those rights, not to save souls. And that is an important distinction.

Adams began with this distinction. Our government was premised on the theory that government is instituted to secure rights, not to save souls. That is some task for another institution in society. Yet, we also have on our currency the motto "In God we trust." In our Pledge of Allegiance we speak of "one nation under God."

This religious orientation of the government is reflected in the Gallup poll that shows that 90 percent of the American public believes in God and 70 percent is affiliated with a church or a sect. Even though they may not be regular attenders, 70 percent of our people are, in fact, affiliated with an organized religion. And so today, as existed two hundred years ago, we have a split. We still have the separationists, the Roger Williamses of Rhode Island, the hard-liners who wish to maintain, as Jefferson did many years after the Constitution was drafted, "a wall of separation." (He penned this phrase in a letter written in the 1800s, so it was not contemporary with the Bill of Rights debate.) Alongside this separationist view is the school of thought known as accommodation, which attempts to bring that creative tension, that delicate balance, between no established church or religion and yet the right to exercise freely one's faith and exercise one's conscience. That schizophrenia, I suggest, has been with us throughout our nation's history.

When we look at the federal Constitution, we may forget that it arose out if a cabal of thirteen states, each of which had its own constitution. New Hampshire's Constitution, the second oldest in the land, dates from 1784. The Massachusetts Constitution is from 1780. And those constitutions, older than the federal, are fascinating because in their Bill of Rights, they also reflect this schizophrenia, this split between establishment and free exercise.

Article 4 of our Bill of Rights in New Hampshire says, "Among the natural rights, some are, by their very nature, inalienable, because no equivalent can be given or received for them. Of this kind are the rights of conscience." Does the state put its money where its mouth is? Yes. According to our New Hampshire Bill of Rights, "no person who is conscientiously scrupulous about bearing arms shall be compelled, thereto." So for us, under our state constitution and in crafting statutes for our state militia (in which I serve as a colonel), we have made it very clear that we do not take anyone who wishes scrupulously, under their conscience, not to bear arms. For us, under our constitution, there is no debate. The Bill of Rights makes it clear.

So religion is exercised freely. At the same time, however, until 1877 the New Hampshire Constitution said that no one could hold public office who was not a Protestant. And the government in the state, as with the other New England states, often exercises its functions in a meetinghouse or a town hall that actually is a church. They are one and the same. For this reason, Congregational churches in New England generally have nothing in the front of the church—no altar, and usually not even a cross. Many of the old churches had a dual function. It was where the folks met in town meeting, and it was also where they met on Sunday for church. For them, separating church and state was something they dealt with more at the conscience level or the thinking level than in terms of actual practice.

That schizophrenia has carried over into the cases the United States Supreme Court has had to deal with. And I suggest to you it is virtually impossible to come up with a test or a rule or a standard that will synthesize some of the things Adams considered in his chapter. According to *Wisconsin* v. *Yoder,* the Amish are free to remove their kids from school before the age of sixteen. They have a religious right to do so. On the other hand, Mormons can have only one wife at a time. Four at a time is unconstitutional. Yet, I cannot think of a reason why that is so. If people, for religious reasons, want to take their kids out of school and want to support four wives, they should be free to do so. But evolving standards have changed—the Mormon case was decided a hundred years ago; the Amish case, within the last fifteen years.

What about unemployment benefits if one does not want to work in a munitions plant? Or some people who work in a factory get shifted over to the munitions side and say that they cannot do that. They like the clause in the New Hampshire constitution about bearing arms and they do not want even to pack or make arms and they go on unemployment. Or can they? Yes, they can, says the Supreme Court. On the other hand, Adams mentioned that one cannot take Saturday off and be given that day off with pay by one's employer, because most people take Sunday off. So, under the case of *Thornton* v. *Calder,* the government will not let one, in one's private employment, have Saturday off with pay.

By a 6-3 vote, as recently as 1983, the United States Supreme Court in the *Marsh* case permitted the chaplain in Nebraska (a good Presbyterian) to be paid $319 a month to make a prayer at the opening of their legislature. And one of the prayers is about as nonneutral as I could find: "Father in heaven, the suffering and death of your son brought life to the whole world, moving our hearts to praise your glory. The power of the cross reveals your concern for the world and the wonder of Christ crucified." Not only Presbyterians but non-Trinitarians or non-Christians serving in the Nebraska legislature paid $319 a month to hear that prayer. On the other hand, the school kids in Alabama cannot have two minutes in total silence to pray or to meditate, by the same 6-3 vote. Is there a guiding principle? Is there a neutral standard of law going through these two cases that were decided just two years apart by the same 6-3 vote?

I suggest that the split continues. University students, by a decisive vote on the Supreme Court, can set up and have religious organizations on state university property. On the other hand, secondary school students were denied this privilege by a 4-4 vote. Where is the neutral principle there? Where is the balance? And how is it being struck in a way that judges across the land will know where to draw the line?

We have, as Adams mentioned, the famous *Walz* case, in which Justice Douglas spoke about tax exemptions for church property. Such exemptions are indeed an indirect aid to religion. Atheists do not get a tax break for their church—they do not have one. But they pay those of us who do go to church. On the other hand, Bob Jones University loses its tax-exempt status because it discriminates on the basis of race, though it is a religious institution. Therefore, not all religions are given tax breaks; it apparently depends on *which* religion gets the tax break.

I suggest that, in looking through the cases, in trying to synthesize a guiding principle, Adams has been able at least to offer a test or a solution. But the Adams-O'Connor test, I suggest, will not answer all of these questions, any more than any other test will. One of the most difficult jobs that any judge has is to balance the creative tension between a pluralistic society, one that is basically religious, albeit in three hundred different directions, and the tendency to have the majority establish a state church or a federal religion. The Supreme Court and the Bill of Rights, of course, are antimajoritarian. They are premeditated and willful institutions to deprive the majority of what it most wants—to require everyone else to accept its religion. In the United States, however, they cannot. So, if Congress or a state voted to establish a church and to fund it and inculcate its values in the population, a very antimajoritarian document, the Bill of Rights, stands in the way.

The nonelected judges, who are appointed for life and who construe the Constitution, have struggled and they have labored. But I suggest that, in giving us the divergent answers they have come up with, they have been unable to define, yet, a coherent view. I appreciate the fact that Judge Adams has, at least, offered us the "accommodation theory." And, hopefully, at some point, we may get a guiding principle that will enable us to understand why school kids cannot have two minutes of silence in Alabama, but the Nebraska legislature gets to pay a Presbyterian minister with government funds to give them the guidance that I am sure we all need.

////Accommodation and the Religious Clauses////

// John F. Wilson, responder////

Judge Adams has made a most valuable contribution in his chapter. I had presumed that he might trace in a relatively conventional fashion the history of how religion has been treated under the Constitution—beginning with the drafting of the two religion clauses of the First Amendment as a kind of afterthought to the Constitution, taking note of the century and a half of their neglect in federal law, culminating in the last four decades of their interpretation and, finally, the contemporary contesting of their meaning. Rather than giving us that potted history, he has chosen to focus our attention on the future—specifically, to reflect on the play between the establishment and free exercise clauses and to propose a formulation for their interaction with respect to a particular range of issues. Thus, although he has counseled us not to neglect the past, the burden of his challenge is to invite us to think about how future church-state law might be developed on the basis of the past that has come to us. This is a most constructive turn.

My response to Adams will take the form of several marginal comments on his chapter. Through this device I hope to focus certain broader issues—especially concerning how law and social policy interact. Conceivably this approach may also stimulate lines of further inquiry and reflection.

My first comment concerns imagery, and more specifically how images work to constrain or to liberate our thought. Of course, one metaphor

has played an immensely important role in thinking about the establishment clause, especially since the *Everson*[1] decision of 1947. In that decision, Justice Black elected to make Thomas Jefferson's image of a wall of
separation normative to interpretation of relations between church and state.
No matter that Jefferson authored the figure in a routine partisan occasional
letter, nor that he seems to have preferred his material walls to be serpen-
tine. No matter also that better relevant images can be located in the writings of the Founders—like James Madison's tracing of a line of separation.
The image of the wall it was, and that formulation has cast a long shadow
over the succeeding four decades.

For Adams, the image of twin beacons as enabling sailors to chart
a course through hazardous waters is a felicitous alternative—better, we
must concur, than Chief Justice Rehnquist's image of Scylla and Charybdis as paired threats, which, aside from the elegance of being a classical reference, seems most unfortunate. Of course, one notable point
about the imagery of twin beacons is that it is dynamic and interactive
rather than static—it suggests the charting of a course by responsible
human agents, rather than the reactive encounter with a static obstacle
in that favored by Justice Black. It also portrays the realm of politics in
terms of statecraft rather than in terms of coping with unnatural forces,
as in the Rehnquist image. So Adams's imagery has by its choice significantly elevated our consideration of these questions.

The imagery of twin beacons also effectively argues against several
recently proposed approaches to interpretation of these clauses. One is
the claim that the two clauses prohibiting establishment and protecting
religious liberty are to be read as one. Surely the anomaly of two clauses
deserves attention—one clause sufficed for other basic rights like free
speech or free assembly. In passing, Adams has indicated good reasons
why the proposal to read the two religion clauses as one does not quite
work. Indeed, the best-known version of the proposal makes the outcome of reading them together a virtual destruction of religion as a cat-
egory suitable for governmental cognizance or protection. Perhaps the
most constructive side of this move to read the clauses as one (and it is
important) has been to argue that religious rights always exist in relationship to other rights—to speech, assembly, and so forth.

---

[1] 330 U.S. 1 (1947).

Another approach implicitly rejected at Adams's hands is the proposal that original intent should guide us in the interpretation of these clauses. Now, there is a sense in which attention to original significance or meaning must be a part of any adequate interpretation of a constitution. But whether we should talk of original intent is another matter—surely original consensus would be better, for it was not a single resolve the clauses captured but a compromise between different resolves. Already this fact suggests that interpretation is required. And to revert to the felicitous imagery of navigating treacherous waters with the aid of beacons, it suggests that, while account must be taken of established points of reference, in the end, safe passage will be effected through contemporary informed judgments. So my first comment is to register strong appreciation for the appropriate imagery Adams proposes.

A second comment concerns the limited reach of the doctrine of "permissible accommodation" that Adams advocates. In developing this concept, it is clear he views this doctrine as made necessary by the expansion of governmental action that impacts upon religion, certainly in unprecedented and perhaps in unanticipated ways. In the drafting of the Bill of Rights, the First Congress could not have conceived of federal regulation of the workweek, or modern governmental dilemmas about defining the beginnings of life or its termination as related to medical treatment. For Adams, this doctrine of permissible accommodation concerns a "zone" created by the expanded reach of government into our lives. That zone exists between, so to speak, claims rooted in free exercise and those in which there is compelling state interest that justifies imposing a burden on religion.

This is a limited or finite range of activity—albeit one that is increasingly significant. But it is only a quadrant of the church-state territory, shall we say, and the doctrine of permissible accommodation directly concerns that area alone. So that, at least as I read Adams, one of the beacons alone, that of free exercise, is sufficient to guide one whole class of transits through perilous waters, and the other, something like the modification of *Everson* as finally codified in the Lemon three-part test, properly guides another. In underscoring what I take to be Adams's attention exclusively to this particular intermediate range of issues, I do not mean to criticize it as a limitation but to welcome it as making explicit distinctions that will surely need to become commonplace. In passing, it is noteworthy that the *Zorach*[2] case becomes the starting point for this doctrine. For *Zorach* is often portrayed as an exhibit of the Court's loss of the courage of its conviction, so to speak, in the face of public outcry over *McCollum*.[3] In the perspective Adams offers, it is the beginning of a positive facing up to the reality of our modern religiously plural society as governmental activity impacts upon it.

Finally, let me underscore what I see as the most basic point Adams makes in his chapter. It is an observation so commonplace as to have lost its power to arrest our attention. In his phrase, it is the *fact* of "increased governmental activity." He has concisely divided the issue, both noting, on the one hand, the range of positive governmental programs that bring federal, state, and local authorities into the lives of citizens in ways unimagined before this century, and, on the other, the potential for government actions to seem to sanction (or not, as the case may be) particular religious beliefs or practices to the detriment of others.

The growth of government and its impact on our lives has been so relentless and steady—and for the most part so necessary and beneficial—that we take it for granted, like the air we breathe. Furthermore, realistically speaking, like the air, we cannot do without it; it is vital to our lives. What is noteworthy for our purposes, however, is how drastically this growth changes the conditions under which government and religion interact. From a condition two hundred years ago in which, it was presumed, religion might concern itself with particulars of daily life but that a new national government had no business so intruding, we have now reached an almost opposite set of conditions, in which government intervention in our lives is taken for granted and the notion that religion should so intrude is almost unthinkable. My comments on this sea change, or long-standing transformation of our society, are only two.

First, I do not believe we can reverse this process. To call attention to this sea change is not to propose we can affect the tides. We can, however, build dikes, reinforce dams, and create jetties that, taken to-

---

[2]343 U.S. 306 (1954).

[3]333 U.S. 206 (1948).

gether, will moderate the actual impact of the rising water. This is exactly what is happening in the area of rights guaranteed under the Constitution, and rights related to the religion clauses have their part to play in this engineering program.

Second, there is a sense in which there is another neglected clause of the Constitution regarding religion and government, namely Article 6, ruling out a religious test for office in the new federal government. In the eyes of the Founders, that was the *basic* clause, one that in its own time was radical, for it set the new federal venture on a different footing than that on which the colonies became states, most of which still held to religious tests for office. Article 6 was not thought sufficient in the course of the debate surrounding ratification, so that the clauses of the First Amendment were crafted to supplement it. In my view, as we seek to understand the work of the Founding Fathers, we need to return to the significance of Article 6, which made the fundamental claim that religious belief and practice should be independent of government action. That, in my view, is the great beacon, to use Judge Adams's image, whose rays are refracted into the twin beacons of which he has spoken.